# The Psychology of Selling and Persuasion

Learn the Real Techniques to Close the Sale Every Time using Proven Principles of Psychology, Manipulation, and Persuasion

Leonard Moore

Copyright © 2019 Leonard Moore

All rights reserved.

In no way is it legal to reproduce, duplicate, or transmit any part of this document in either electronic means or in printed format. recording of this publication is strictly prohibited and any storage of this document is not allowed unless with written permission from the publisher. all rights reserved. The information provided herein is stated to be truthful and consistent, in that any liability, in terms of inattention or otherwise, by any usage or abuse of any policies, processes, or directions contained within is the solitary and utter responsibility of the recipient reader. under no circumstances will any legal responsibility or blame be held against the publisher for any reparation, damages, or monetary loss due to the information herein, either directly or indirectly. Respective authors own all copyrights not held by the publisher. The information herein is offered for informational purposes solely, and is universal as so. the presentation of the information is without contract or any type of guarantee assurance. The trademarks that are used are without any consent, and the publication of the trademark is without permission or backing by the trademark owner. all trademarks and brands within this book are for clarifying purposes only and are the owned by the owners themselves, not affiliated with this document. The author wishes to thank 123RF / peshkova for the image on the cover.

# TABLE OF CONTENTS

Free Bonus: 3 Insanely Effective Words To Hypnotize Anyone In A Conversation ................................................................. 6

Introduction ............................................................................. 8

Chapter 1: Setting the Table ................................................. 10
    Goal Setting ..................................................................... 10
    Make your Action Goals SMART .................................... 11
    Habit Stacking to Implement Needed Changes in Behavior ........ 13
    Principles of Persuasion ................................................... 15
    Setting Your System ........................................................ 19

Chapter 2: Loading the Funnel ............................................. 24
    Always Be in Contact ...................................................... 24
    Selling is a Continuous Process ........................................ 28
    Always Have Something to Give ..................................... 32

Chapter 3: Getting in the Door .............................................. 38
    Do Your Research ............................................................ 39
    Don't Sell ......................................................................... 42
    Assume the Meeting ........................................................ 43
    Developing Solutions ...................................................... 47
    Assessing Needs .............................................................. 51
    Debriefing Yourself ......................................................... 54
    Productizing your Offerings ............................................ 56

Chapter 4: Killing the Presentation ....................................... 58
    It's Not Logical; It's Emotional ....................................... 58
    Emotions and the Principles of Persuasion ...................... 60
    Pre-Planning for Objection .............................................. 63
    Learn What the Competition Says ................................... 67

Chapter 5: Negotiating the Deal ............................................ 70
    Evaluating Your Options ................................................. 70
    Dealing with Objection .................................................... 72
    Assume the Sale ............................................................... 79

Chapter 6: Closing and Reselling .......................................... 82
    Building Your Customer Relationships ........................... 82
    Expand the Relationship .................................................. 85
    Get the Referral ............................................................... 89

- Chapter 7: Your Sales Script Framework ............................... 94
  - Key Points Worksheet ............................................... 94
  - Breaking down the Process .......................................... 95
  - Writing Your Scripts ................................................ 97
  - The Sales Funnel ................................................... 98
  - Example Script ..................................................... 103
  - The Script ......................................................... 105
  - Wrapping Up ....................................................... 109
- Conclusion ............................................................. 110
- Other Books by Leonard Moore .......................................... 112

## Free Bonus:
## 3 Insanely Effective Words to Hypnotize Anyone in a Conversation

If you're trying to persuade and convince other people then words are the most important tool you absolutely have to master.

As humans we interact with words, we shape the way we think through words, we express ourselves through words. Words evoke feelings and have the ability to talk to the listener's subconscious.

In this free guide you'll discover 3 insanely effective words that you can easily use to start hypnotizing anyone in a conversation.

Go to **http://eepurl.com/cRTY5X** to download the free guide

# Introduction

As long as people have had goods to sell, sales have been a part of the marketplace. Over the past hundred years, the sales profession has changed from an art to a science. Decades of research into human behavior has been leveraged into finding the answer to one question: What makes humans buy something?

There is no magic wand you can wave to cause people to do what you ask them to do, but there are certain responses and behaviors that research has suggested are hard-wired into our brains over years of evolution. In this book, we distill much of this research in human behavior down to actionable steps that you can take to improve your selling abilities.

Whether you are a sales professional, a business owner who needs to increase sales in your company, or someone looking to build a successful sales system, this book will help you to understand the latest thinking in the psychology of selling and persuasion. We'll look at the principles of persuasion, selling strategies, and negotiating techniques designed to help you close more sales and delight your customers after the sale.

In the end, we'll take these ideas and show you how to script a simple, effective sales process that will help you to systemize the principles we'll cover in this book.

There are many books on sales, and we would like to thank you for reading this one. We hope you find it helpful and valuable to your sales efforts. If you enjoy the book, make sure to leave a short review on Amazon. We would love to hear your thoughts.

# Chapter 1:
## Setting the Table

**Goal Setting**

Before you start to build, improve, or remake your sales efforts, you need to set down a target. You need to develop tangible, achievable goals that you'll be aiming for with your new sales outlook. The persuasion techniques that we'll talk about later in this book won't mean anything if you don't take the time to develop a good road map to where you're going. That map is developed by setting goals.

Now is a good time to take a moment and decide what you really want to achieve and evaluate where you are right now. According to goal setting master Jim Rohn, you should take a moment with pen and paper and write out what's important to you and where you are on each of those points. After you've made these notes, take a moment to reflect on your current position in each of these instances and decide if you're happy with that level, or if you would like to improve it.

Once you have this baseline assessment, it's much easier to know what you need to do to reach your desired level of achievement on each of the points you decide are important. You'll have a benchmark that you can come back to as you move forward, evaluating your current efforts as they relate to your goal road map. By putting a definition to your goals in this way, you can make them achievable by creating a step-by-step plan to reach each one.

Don't be afraid to dream big here! The bigger the goal, the more steps it may take to reach, but each of those tasks will be something you can do. When all of the small tasks are taken together, you'll have the steps you need to reach that big goal.

For our purposes here, take one more pass through this list of goals and current baselines and answer this question: How will increasing your sales performance help you reach each of those goals? Because, to increase your sales performance, you not only need the tools but you need the motivation to use the tools every day to make those goals a reality. Your overall goal road map will provide that motivation.

**Make your Action Goals SMART**

Now that you know where you are on your journey, and you have a good idea where you're going, it's time to start planning the steps you can take right now to achieve your sales success, and reach your personal goals. We'll call these smaller milestones your Action Goals.

These action goals are meant to be the small, achievable steps that will get you closer to your end goals. You've written those goals down in the previous step, and you've assessed where you are right now in your journey. Now, we'll decide what the first step is for each. Where you are encouraged to be grand with your main goals, with your

Action Goals, we want to pick actions that are SMART — Specific, Measurable, Attainable, Relevant and Time-Related. Jot down some ideas on what you can do next regarding your sales efforts, and let's evaluate those ideas against this framework.

### *Specific*

First, is your Action Goal Specific? When you have a little more room to dream when you are setting your big goals, your Action Goals need to have specificity to them. Instead of "I want to increase my prospecting calls," you should nail it down to "I will make ten additional prospecting calls each week." This is important because you need something that you can measure.

### *Measurable*

A Measurable goal is exactly what it sounds like. It's something you can take a measuring stick to and see how it stacks up against the desired outcome. In our example above, the number 10 is an easy measurement. You look at your call sheet and count the prospecting calls each week. Are you doing ten more? If not, it's easy to see you have some work to do.

### *Attainable*

Your Action Goals must also be Attainable. Nothing will ruin your progress toward your goals more than selecting an Action Goal that is completely out of your reach. This is one of the reasons that you need to make these goals Specific and Measurable. It makes it easier to evaluate whether or not the goal is attainable.

### *Relevant*

It may seem obvious, but your Action Goals need to be relevant to the larger goal they are meant to get you closer to. Can you lay out a step-by-step pathway to the larger goal where your Action Goal is one of the steps?

### *Time-Related*

The final part of the SMART evaluation framework deals with Time. Because we're looking for goals that can be easily evaluated against an objective measurement stick, we naturally are concerned with how long it will take to achieve this goal. So put an estimated time frame on your Action Goal. If it's too long, break it up into shorter steps.

We want to end up with a series of steps that you are going to take today, knowing exactly what you are going to do to accomplish them and be able to measure when they are completed. These Action Goals should be SMART enough to list on a piece of paper and check off when reached.

The Action Goals should not be something you check off and forget about. To reach your larger goal targets, you are going to need to climb their one step at a time. Once you raise to each step, your only direction should be up, so there your action steps need to lead to new habits that become your new baseline for taking the next step.

## Habit Stacking to Implement Needed Changes in Behavior

To help you lock in these improved habits, here's a little self-persuasion technique known as 'habit stacking.' Persuading yourself can be difficult to do since a decision forced on you is rarely effective long-term. When we talk more about the principles of persuasion in the next section, you'll see that the most effective persuasion sets up a situation where another person is more likely to come to their own conclusions because of the path you've put them on. Persuasion doesn't work if your guidance becomes obvious, or your persuasion techniques become overt.

Because of this, it's difficult to persuade yourself into doing something that involves long-lasting change without finding a way to make it more of a subconscious transition. When you need to convince yourself to change your behavior, habit stacking becomes a powerful tool for self-persuasion.

Everyone has habits that they do almost without thinking about them. Take your morning routine, for instance. You probably set your alarm for the same time every day. You may get up, start the coffee, brush your teeth, hit the shower, and so on until you're out the door. When you hit the office, you probably do something very similar almost every day as well. These various habits are locked into our brains by a process called 'neuron pruning.' During our lifetimes, our brain works to make thought as streamlined as possible. When we do something over and over again, the brain devotes neuron 'hard wiring' to those habits, so it doesn't need to keep recreating the connections over and over.

Meanwhile, neurons are taken away from connections that we rarely make. You order fries with your burger, but not a salad. Your brain makes that connection easier and easier, so it takes less work to make that connection in the future.

To lock in your new behavior, find a way to tie it to something you already do. Once you lock the two behaviors together, your brain will help you make the connections automatic over time.

In our prospecting call example, let's say your current habit is to make your prospecting calls before lunch. You make a few calls and then grab something to eat. Use that habit to tie in a specific number, so now you only head to lunch after five prospecting calls. If your old weekly number was ten per week, you could see that being in the habit of five right before lunch will have you far above that total in short order. How can you tie *your* Action Goals to things you already do?

**Principles of Persuasion**

Dr. Robert Cialdini launched a revolution in persuasion studies in the 1984 book *Influence: The Psychology of Persuasion*. Although research had been done on persuasion for decades, Dr. Cialdini's book distilled everything down to six core principles that drive persuasion. He found that some combination of these six principles (and later a seventh principle that he added) were behind most all human persuasion. And what did Dr. Cialdini use as his initial laboratory for research? Sales jobs that he worked on.

It should come as no surprise that the six principles have found a home among sales trainers. What we will do in this book is to show you various points throughout the sales process where you can apply these research-backed principles of persuasion to pull your prospects along the road to becoming customers. Plus, we'll add the seventh principle that Dr. Cialdini added in 2016 in his book *Pre-Suasion*. To get us started, here are the shorthand versions of each principle that we will use to take your sales to the next level.

*Reciprocity*

The first principle is Reciprocity. It's a fairly simple principle based on trading favors. When somebody does a favor for you, you will notice that you try and do them a favor when you get the chance.

It turns out that behavior is something hard-wired into our human brain. It makes world trade work on a larger scale, and on a small scale, it creates the concept of "scratch my back and I'll scratch yours." The fine point on this principle is that once you've given something to someone, they are going to be looking for a way to give you something in return.

In sales, this means finding ways to give your prospect something of value, so they are more likely to give you a sale in return.

## *Scarcity*

The principle of Scarcity is used in marketing and sales all of the time. When we are presented with something that is in short supply, it turns out our brains want that thing even more.

Maybe this helped in our survival way back when pushing us to gather food and shelter while we could so we had resources when they weren't so plentiful. Whatever the reason, research has shown time and time again that people will attach a higher value to something that seems limited.

In one study, researchers put a dozen cookies in a clear jar, and then put only a few of the same cookies in another jar. Test subjects were asked to taste the cookies and tell them which one they liked more. Which jar do you suppose they overwhelmingly chose?

## *Authority*

People like to move in groups and be accepted, so you'll notice that a few of the principles of persuasion deal with doing what is expected or approved. The principle of Authority is one of those based on approval.

In this case, people have been found to respect the opinion of someone they feel has special knowledge or authority over someone who doesn't. For instance, Dr. Cialdini cites one study that had people ask strangers to give them change for the parking meter. One group of testers wore a uniform; the other group just wore normal street clothes. The uniformed researchers were much more likely to get the strangers to give them change for the meter than the normally dressed requesters.

## *Consistency*

The principle of Consistency also has its roots in the desire of humans to 'fit in.' The principle states that people like to do things that are 'consistent' with whom they believe they are or whom they want to be.

This principle is also the backing for people keeping their commitments. Once we say we're going to do something, we are more likely to do it.

While there are plenty of ways to use this principle to increase sales, we should also mention that Consistency is a great self-persuasion tool as well. If you commit to someone else that you are going to change a certain behavior, you are giving yourself a leg up on accomplishing that change, because you'll want to keep your word.

## *Liking*

I feel that this principle is probably one of the more intuitive to understand, but it's important to detail it here because it is of such importance in persuasion. The principle of Liking simply means that we are more likely to do things for people we like than those we don't.

Politics is probably the most visible ongoing experiment in the principle of liking. While people would like to think that they research people they vote into office, in reality, people tend to vote for people they like. Say things people like to hear, get elected. Whether you ever do those things is another matter. Politicians are most concerned not with getting things done, but with being popular with their constituents so they can get elected again.

*Consensus*

Consensus could be described as 'majority rules.' Once again, we see how people want to fit in with other people.

The principle of Consensus tells us that people are most likely to look at the behavior of others if they are trying to come to a decision.

The most popular study in this area was based on trying to get hotel guests to reuse their towels rather than change them out every day. Studies found that about 75 percent of people tend to reuse a towel during their stay. When the hotel just left a card in the bathroom telling people that 75 percent of their guests reused their towels, reuse went up by over 25 percent. Environmental appeals about reduced washing didn't even compare. People do what others do.

*Unity*

The final persuasion principle is Unity. As mentioned earlier, Dr. Cialdini added this principle nearly three decades after his original six principles, but it is important. This principle says that people are more likely to help people who are 'one of them.'

For illustration, we can look again at politics, where persuasion is the name of the game. How often do you see politicians visit with potential voters and try to 'fit in' with the audience? They'll eat at a favorite local diner or stress their similarities with people in the community no matter where they are speaking.

Politicians do this because research has shown that people tend to go along with others who share a commonality with them. In negotiation studies, for instance, agreements have been found much more quickly when one of the negotiators starts the proceedings by stressing what the two sides have already agreed to.

## Setting Your System

Now that we've got the basics of persuasion out of the way, we're almost ready to get into building your sales through these powerful tools. But before we get started, there are just a few more pre-planning items we need to take care of to make sure we are ready to take off quickly.

### *Building Your Communication System*

To make sure that your persuasion efforts turn into maximum sales, we need to make sure that you have a system in place to enable your efforts to turn into conversions. The lead part of that system is communication.

Communication has never been more vital than today. Your customers expect you to be always on, always available, 24 hours a day, seven days a week. The Internet makes always-on communication not only possible but expected. The principle of Liking almost necessitates that you do everything you can to live up to your customers' expectations as much as possible so that you can keep them delighted.

We can't be 'on call' all day, every day, but in this digital world, there are more options than ever for a little computerized assistance that can pay dividends in augmenting your work. There are too many systems out there to list in this book, but suffice it to say there are plenty of ways you can automate your process and communication.

The main thing you need to do is first define the way you like to work and then look for the tools that will add to that process. Here are a couple of key areas you should look for help:

## Automation

The tools you look for should offer as much automation for your everyday tasks as possible. Do you send a 'thank you' email after initial meetings? Do you have an onboarding welcome email that you send to every new customer? Do you need to set up a lead report for each new contact? These and other types of repetitive actions are things that can all be easily taken care of by automation software.

## Stay out of the way

No matter what you choose, it shouldn't take you longer to set up than it would take to do the task by hand. Also, look for tools that don't make you change your system just to accommodate the software.

### *Ready You're Process*

Now is also a great time to take a look at your sales process and make sure it works the way you want it. If there are things you would like to change, paperwork you would like to streamline, or new packages you would like to put together, now is the opportunity to put those ideas together.

Another thing to think about is putting milestones into your process. These are points in the sales cycle that would trigger the next phase in the journey. These points will be another key part of your automation process, as you can key certain automated activities to those key points. This breaking down of the process is similar to breaking down your large goals into smaller pieces. Tasks are easier to deal with than working with the big picture as a whole.

Jot down all of these ideas and hold them for now. Let's move on to our next planning point on the list.

## *Plan Your "Always Yes" Ask*

Here's the next part of your planning that takes advantages of the persuasion principles. The principle of Reciprocity says that people are more likely to give you something if you first give them something. So, let's spend some time while we're looking at the sales process to find some 'freebies' to give your prospects. Your giveaways don't necessarily need to be something that costs money. Think about informational products that you can put together that would be valuable to your clients. Even better would be something that could be delivered digitally. And think about partnering with other companies that are complementary to what you offer. What would they provide for you to give a potential client introduction for their salesperson?

Meanwhile, the Consistency principle says that people tend to act consistently with the way they have acted or committed to acting in the past. One of the places you can take advantage of this principle is to find places along the sales cycle where you can get the client to say "yes" when it's easy so that when it comes time to make the presentation, they will be more committed to saying "yes" when it counts.

Asking the client if they would like to receive your various freebie items is one way to combine both of these principles into an easy "yes." A small regular event, like an informational presentation with lunch included for a few clients at a local lunch spot, is another possibility for an easy ask to provide value and get a "yes" at the same time.

Put down all of the ideas that come to you for now and come back to them once you've gone through the rest of this book. You may even have some additions that you make to these initial plans as we talk more about the other parts of the sales process. We'll be applying the principles of persuasion to improve the entire process, and you may have more ideas along the way.

The main effort here was not only to lay the foundation for your new sales process, but also to apply the principles of persuasion to *you*. At this point, you should be getting energized and thinking about the possibilities of what you can grow your sales into with some new thinking about your process and some strategic application of the power of persuasion and the psychology of selling.

Let's dig in.

# Chapter 2:
## Loading the Funnel

**Always Be in Contact**

People have often said that sales are a numbers game. Put enough leads in the pipeline, and eventually, sales will come out of the other end. That's only partially true.

In most cases, sales is a *contact* game; not the kind of contact where you need a helmet (hopefully!), but the kind of contact that keeps you in regular communication with your clients and potential clients. In this chapter, we'll talk about how to keep in contact with your prospects and clients, so that your sales funnel is always full of potential deals just waiting for you to close them.

***The Most Important Sales Call***

No matter what you're selling, there is no more important contact that you will make with a prospective customer than the *first* contact. Sometimes known as a "cold call," this first contact is the toughest part of the job for most salespeople. Sure, there are several important points in a sales cycle, but where you need to be on your A-game is when you first make contact with a new client.

If you are selling in a system that gives you warm leads to work from, congratulations! Most sales professionals don't have that luxury, especially in highly competitive industries or markets. What your company has given you is a gift, and you should take it and run.

Warm leads are contacts where a customer has requested contact because they are ready to buy. They are just trying to decide where. That is a long way down the funnel, so you have an advantage toward moving into a sale.

But, that doesn't mean that your first contact is any less important. It could be argued that your first customer meeting is even *more* important since much more work has already been done for you. It would be a shame to fumble the client contact when you are already this close to winning.

For those of you who have leads that are simply names on a list, you may have more work to do to convert the sale, but your first call is even more important to your success. Without getting that lead to at least start the journey with you, you are out of luck.

Either way, understanding the principles of persuasion and being able to put them to work for you is vital for any first customer contact. Don't waste your first impression. Use it instead to set up your success.

The easiest first call persuasion tactic is to use Reciprocity. Find something that you can give to the customer in the first few seconds of the call; if you make the whole purpose of that first contact about giving the customer something, even better. Your generosity will set them up to give you something in return later in this call or the next, and the thing you are looking for is an agreement to meet again. That "yes" also begins to lay the groundwork for Consistency, getting the customer to start a history of agreeing with you.

The whole point of this first contact should be to get the customer to like you, and the easiest way to do that on the first contact is not to waste their time. Since the first contacts usually happen on your schedule and not the customer's, you should respect their time.

Even if you are selling something that is fairly low cost, where your first contact might be the opening to a single sales call, you still need to establish Liking right up front. It may be the only way to keep the customer talking to you.

No matter the situation, the last thing you want to do in your opening contact is to try and sell. Instead, use some quick efforts at persuasion to keep the conversation moving to the next step.

### *The Importance of Follow-Up*

If the first contact is the most important part of the sales cycle, then follow up is the second. Before you leave the first contact stage, your effort should be to do no more than setting up a commitment for the follow-up.

Recapping quickly on what we've done so far setting up your persuasion track, you'll note we've already talked about the principle of Consistency, and how important it is to get the client moving in your direction. Setting up Reciprocity by giving something early also puts you in a good position for success on your next contact as well. Thanks to these early persuasion techniques you've implemented, the follow-up should be an easy next step.

Depending on your product and situation, your follow-up could take several different forms. Next are some ideas on where you could head during the follow-up. Consistency and Reciprocity both suggest that this is a good time to ask for your first "yes." Not a big ask, but something the customer can agree to, followed by permission to schedule an in-depth needs analysis.

## *Position Yourself as an Ongoing Resource*

By positioning yourself as a resource for your customer, you will accomplish two things where persuasion is concerned. First, you can continue the Consistency principle that you've started in your first contact by continuing to provide value for your client. Once they build a habit of depending on you for your expertise, they will start to make you the first call for any questions they have in your industry. This status puts you first in line for the new business going forward. Even if the client calls you for a solution that you don't provide, it's better to get to make that decision. Who doesn't want the "right of first refusal" on new business?

With Consistency established with this customer, when you do have something you can sell them, they will already be primed for the "yes." Here's where the investment in persuasion pays off. Customers who buy before are more likely to continue to buy from you, without reinvesting more time.

Next, you can use the persuasion principle of Authority through your ongoing contact by making *yourself* the authority. Building your profile with your clients by passing on interesting information, new product tips and demos on products you think could help them will make your recommendations be the deciding factor in future buying choices. Even if the information you give doesn't directly have anything to do with the product you sell, making yourself an authority in the space will make sure that you know anytime the customer is ready to make a purchase. That early contact will give you a chance to make alternative or complementary suggestions from your product line.

## Selling is a Continuous Process

Selling is not so much of an individual task as it is a continuous process. While you may be finishing a sale with one client, you may also be making the first contact with some new prospects and checking in with your existing customers. Here are some thoughts on managing the constantly moving sales cycle.

### *Use Your Contact to Uncover Needs*

As sales professionals know, you need to be in contact early and often in your prospect's sales journey. Early contact is important from a persuasion standpoint as well. The best time to use your persuasion techniques is during the initial part of the sales cycle so that you can have things moving your way by the time the customer is ready to write the check.

Keeping in contact at the early part of the sales funnel also allows you to find additional needs that may change the sale in your favor or give you an additional sale with add-ons or upgrades.

Your sales process should include a lot of listening and just enough talking to keep the conversation going. Information is the absolute gold you're looking to uncover if you are going to be able to take maximum advantage of your persuasion opportunities.

The problem is that most people don't naturally give up information or talk at all without prodding. The key to keeping the other side of the conversation going is to talk as little as possible, giving important information and asking open-ended questions.

Many salespeople like to talk and this works against you. Learn to listen and react to what your client is telling you about their needs. No two people buy for the same reasons, and by listening to the needs of each particular customer, you can use the principles of persuasion to your best ability.

## *Address Needs and Position Yourself as the Expert*

Perfecting your abilities as a strong listener allows you to address the needs of your customer head-on, instead of only finding out about a particular question your client may have when you get down to signing the check.

In addition to answering the customer's concern and removing barriers to the sale, you can also use these opportunities to engage persuasion more in your favor. Let's take a look at each of the persuasion principles and see where they can be effectively applied to addressing the needs of your customer and moving them farther down the funnel toward the sale.

### Reciprocity

Remembering that the principle of Reciprocity says that you are more likely to get something back if you first give something of value, taking the time to thoroughly address concerns will earn you a lot of payback later in the sales process. Make sure that you highlight your desire to take care of their questions and not rush them into a decision without all of the facts. This attention to making them feel comfortable will translate into more willingness to move through the final sales process quickly later.

### Scarcity

Many times, you will have the ability to note how a particular feature or benefit of your product is something only your offering provides. Being the only one to offer an answer to a question or need that the customer has can give you a real 'no brainer' status on the list of possible choices.

But how can you use Scarcity if your offering isn't the best at addressing a customer concern? Focus the conversation on the scarcity of a certain price or availability to push past the reluctance to accept your answer. "We offer solid performance on that point, similar to most everybody in the market, but this limited time pricing offer makes us by far the best value if you make your purchase now."

## Authority

When your customer comes up with questions, you should have facts and information from third-party sources whenever possible. Keeping a virtual clipping file that you can email at a moment's notice is great for showing what industry publications and well-known customers have said about your product, especially in situations that directly address the customer's question.

Read trade magazines and set web clipper alerts for various questions that you get asked often and collect authoritative answers that will back you up on key points.

## Consistency

Have some options at the ready to address concerns during the sales cycle. Presenting these options as a question of "which will work better for you" will keep the customer selecting you and your product. There is no wrong answer in this type of scenario since it is merely a choice of *how* they wish to buy, not *if*. "I understand you need for more capacity. We have an option for larger 7-gallon and 12-gallon tanks. Which would work best for you?" Selecting either one is saying "yes" again, which is a pattern you want to reinforce at every step.

Liking

One of the more obvious points, but treating the client with the kind of respect they appreciate will only make you like them more. A purchase can be a high-stress time for many people, especially when the dollar amount is large. Never lose track of that, and use your answers to questions to make the customer feel that they are being thoughtful in their decision-making, letting them know that you appreciate the time they are putting into making the right decision.

Consensus

Here it's good to have your clipping file at the ready to show what "most people" do in similar situations. Subconsciously, people want to be part of the crowd. Use opportunities to reinforce that with answers to questions. "Most of my customers go with the three-year service plan to cover that type of use." "The company sells the 72-inch wide version almost three-to-one because a lot of people need that same capacity."

Unity

Make sure that you take time during this part of the process to point out where the customer is thinking like you, highlighting how you are similar to the customer. The principle of Unity says that people tend to buy from people that are "like them," so use questions and concerns to highlight that. "I went with that same model when I bought mine." "I wondered that, too, so I did a little digging in the specs and here's what I found." Always try to point out that you are on their side in this process.

### *Prospect, Sell, Follow Up*

As long as your customer is in the decision-making process, they are in the funnel and still moving toward a potential sale. This thinking is what's behind that well-worn adage of 'prospect, sell, and follow-up.' In the days of limited information, expensive travel and difficult contact, the salesman who won the sale was often the guy or gal who showed up over and over and over again.

Today is a different story. Your customer is inundated with contact from a variety of sources all day, every day. Just making contact isn't enough anymore. Every sales pro, including your competition, can do that easily while making your customer feel like they don't want to think about this decision anymore. But you can't lose contact with the customer and potentially lose the sale to someone else. Follow-up is still highly important to closing the sale. It just needs to be done with persuasion in mind.

Sales guru Jill Konrath agrees with this need to re-think the follow-up system you may be using and work to add value to each contact. Her tips include re-iterating the value your product or service will bring to their situation, sharing thoughts and insights you may have had regarding the customer's situation since your last meeting, and using your repeat contact opportunities to educate your customer further.

I find that education is the one thing that you can always offer your customer that adds value for the customer while giving you further persuasion advantages. Educating the customer further cements your Authority with the customer, gives you a Reciprocity advantage, and builds Liking for you, to name just a few of the persuasive points. So, let's take a moment to focus on how you can make education work for you to close the sale.

**Always Have Something to Give**

Because follow-up and continued customer education can add such persuasive punch to your sales process, it's important to be thinking about this before you ever make your first prospecting call. It's vital to have resources that you have planned to use for this purpose, just as it will be important that you continue to build these resources on a regular basis so that you always have something to give.

In the remainder of this chapter, we'll talk about some ideas of what you can develop at little to no cost. No matter what cooperation your company may or may not give you, you can still create value for your customers to keep them moving toward the sale.

### *Organize Events or Meet-ups*

Michael Port, in his best-seller *Book Yourself Solid,* made a point of advising readers to "always have something to invite people to." He said that this one change in his sales strategy doubled his business inside of a year.

Principles of persuasion tell us that Reciprocity is important to foster in our customers, and giving something helps to get something later in return. This is one of the reasons that having events to invite people to regularly is a low-cost or no-cost way to give your customers something of value that will undoubtedly have a positive impact on your business. Who doesn't like to be invited to something relevant to them or their business?

What kind of event could you create? Imagination is the key. The most obvious is the open house night to allow customers to get hands on your products or get expert advice on how to use them. If you sell forklifts, you could invite clients to come and try out some of the inventory in the warehouse or the parking lot. If you sell gas grills and outdoor cooking equipment, you could invite a local barbecue chef in to give some cooking tips and make some food. (Everybody shows up for free food!)

Meet-ups are free and easy to set up. Come up with a topic related to your business and set a Meet-up date for a local restaurant's banquet room for lunch. Open it up to the public on Meetup.com and promote it to all of your customers. You might end up with new prospective customers you haven't met yet! You might want to pick up the tab for a couple of key customers to come; most will pay their own way for the chance to learn more about the subject you're speaking about.

Meetings don't have to be in person, either. Consider webinars and conference calls or even recorded video presentations that you've held previously. And of these ideas and many others would be an opportunity to keep in contact with a prospective customer without needing to push the sale. All the while, you not only increase Reciprocity in your side of the ledger but you also further your Authority and Liking persuasion as well.

### *Develop Resources*

Developing your educational resources doesn't need to cost anything more than your time if you can manage the word processing program or presentation software. If you're not a wizard with this type of thing, you can get help relatively inexpensively from online job sites like Fiverr, Upwork and Freelancer. Just put some notes together with what you want and send them off. Once created, you only need to keep these items updated to keep them current and valuable to use time and time again.

What types of things could you produce? Keep notes on questions you hear from customers regularly, and come up with information to answer the questions. Then, find unique ways to put this information into a form that you can easily distribute via email or a download site like Dropbox or Google Drive. Powerpoint slides can be combined with your voice to create an informative video. Typing up a print report can be formatted into a professional looking PDF white paper or even a short book that will be perfect to pass out to customers.

There are even options for creating micro websites for free, such as Google Sites, allowing you to assemble a website page quickly by dragging and dropping various elements around a page. If you can set up a Powerpoint slide, you've got this. Spreadsheets, charts, artwork, audio; almost anything you can think of can be created and distributed digitally.

You don't even need to go to this much effort for everything. Almost anything can be a valuable resource for a customer if it answers a question. Making a habit of checking the web every day for interesting articles may give you just the opening you need to send an email to a customer that day. "I know you've been trying to decide on which model to go with, and I just saw this article on the 9000 that I thought might give you some more good information."

## *Partner with Other Businesses for Gifts and Perks*

In your contact with customers, you are bound to run into other products and services that they are also buying that complement your product. Keep track of these other companies who don't compete with you, but sell to the same customers. Make contact with these other companies and offer to partner up to help both of you. If they have information or discounts that you can give to your new customers, work with them to pass on these leads to their salespeople. While you're at it, offer some of the giveaway items that you've developed for an opportunity to talk to their customers as well.

Working in partnership with other non-competing businesses can be a win-win for both of you, plus it gets more valuable information to your customers and gives you another reason to make contact during the sales process. From a persuasion standpoint, showing cooperation from other businesses elevates your profile as an expert even more and shows consensus with other members of the industry. Passing on information from another company can provide their indirect approval to show your prospective client that others respect your business as well.

# Chapter 3:
## Getting in the Door

We talk a lot about the sales process during this book, but the length of that process may be vastly different depending on the type of product you're selling. Selling yard services will take far less time than selling someone a new house or piece of industrial equipment. The process is the same in both situations; it just has a different timeline.

As we go through these various steps, you'll need to adapt the techniques to your specific situation. You'll find that it's well worth the effort, and hopefully, these ideas will fuel your creativity to come up with specific ideas that work in your day-to-day sales process, no matter what that might be.

Later in this book, we'll reduce much of what we're discussing now into a customized sales script that you'll be able to use as the basis for each new opportunity. Until then, we'll continue to lay the foundations needed for persuasion at each point in a typical sales cycle.

Most of what we've been talking about up to this point has been preparation. Now we're going to start focusing more on what you need to do to use the resources you've developed, along with the initial persuasion foundations you've laid, to start qualifying and completing the sale. Let's set that first sales appointment and get in the door.

**Do Your Research**

This whole chapter is about setting your first appointment and getting in the door for one simple reason: It may be the most important part of the whole sales cycle from the standpoint of persuasion. Salespeople have the opportunity to ruin their persuasive prospects during the initial contact with a customer than at any other time in the sales cycle.

Why? Because your prospect has nothing else to base their view of you and your company on than the initial contact they have with you. Your marketing and advertising campaigns can all be dashed in a moment if your interaction isn't on point. Numerous studies have shown over time that people value their interactions with other people far over any other research or previous information they may have gathered. In short, people put the highest importance on what they learn directly from other people, including how those people make them feel.

This first contact, looking for an appointment, is crucial in setting the right tone for the rest of the sales cycle, so don't rush into it. Before you pick up the phone or drop by in person, do a little research. If the customer has already filled out information on a lead form, take the time to read it and familiarize yourself with the customer. Learn something about the neighborhood your customer is in, or if you sell to other businesses, learn about their customers and the competition. You need to have at least a basic knowledge of your customer before you talk to them so you can relate to their problems.

### *Selling is Problem Solving*

The best salespeople focus on solving problems for their customers. Because of that, you should be looking to establish a conversation with your prospective customer from that first call.

If the customer reached out to you initially, then thank them for contacting you and find out what prompted that initial call. Are they experiencing specific problems? For instance, are they looking for ways to more efficiently handle their service people in the field? Or is their need more general in nature, such as looking for ways to save on their energy bill or get more output from their equipment?

If you're cold calling or following up from a cold call, find out more about the problems the customer faces every day. Cold calls are difficult because you are interrupting your prospect's day, so be as courteous as possible while also trying to start the discussion.

Work on raising problems during that first call by being a good listener. Few people won't take the opportunity to lay out their problems to a sympathetic ear. You might ask how their day's been going or start the discussion by talking about problems you have seen your other customers have recently.

The principles of persuasion can be put to work even here. Using the principle of Unity, talk briefly about the problems you've been working on for other customers or stress your understanding of problems that they mention. Build Consensus by letting the customer know what other customers have done in similar situations and greet their problems with confidence in solutions you could find for them to build Authority. And use Consistency by finding a way to get at least one 'yes' from the customer during this initial call, even if it's only an agreement for another calling time to get more information.

There is only one thing you are working at selling during this initial contact and that is a commitment to the next contact. To make sure the customer follows through on that commitment, offer something of value for the next meeting. We've already prepared some of these valuable items during our preparation, so pick something to use here to entice your customer to commit to your next meeting. In addition to making sure the client will actually keep the commitment, you're also setting up Reciprocity right from the start of the next meeting.

## *Understanding the Customer's Mindset*

This first contact is also a good opportunity to find where the customer is at mentally. Maybe they have several problems they're trying to solve, and you're one of many people they have called for help. Maybe they already view your company as an expert solution to a specific problem they are trying to solve. In the case of a cold call, the customer might not think they have any pressing problems or they might have a problem for which they didn't realize there was help available.

Starting this initial conversation is a good way to find out the baseline that you'll be working from to convert this prospect into a sale. You will also begin to find out some important information on the type of persuasion techniques you'll need to use during the process.

The most effective persuasion techniques are those that lead the customer to reach their own conclusions. When people talk of hating salespeople, what they mean is that they don't like to be 'sold.' No one likes to feel like they are being forced or manipulated into doing something that they don't want to do. By finding where the customer is at the beginning of your sales process, you can find what types of information will be most useful to them so that they can reach a decision. The only time a customer feels forced into a decision is when they are asked to choose before they have gotten enough information to decide on their own.

While you have the customer's attention, ask questions that are geared toward finding what they don't know about your company or their problem, and make notes on what you'll need to accomplish as you move forward. Finding a way to answer all of the customer's questions will be the ultimate key to making the sale.

**Don't Sell**

Perhaps the most important thing to stress at this point is that you should *not* be selling. You should be *listening*. When we talk about building a sales script later in this book, we'll be talking about building a framework to guide your process, but we won't be building a word-for-word dialog for you to use to magically make the sale.

The reason for this is that every customer is different, and therefore, every customer's *problem* is different. There is no magic incantation that you can use on a customer to drive them toward a sale. The principles of persuasion offer as close to a formula as anyone can get to make a sale, but the exact process is adaptive. Persuasion principles can provide some powerful tools to bring your customer to an ultimate decision, but tools are not an answer in and of themselves. Finding the problems and concerns that each customer is facing will give you the best plan to achieve the sale.

If you aren't 'selling' by pushing for a decision, and you're listening to what the customer needs instead, you'll find that the sales job actually gets easier. With your assistance, the customer will lead you to the sale.

That doesn't mean your job as a salesperson isn't important or that the product sells itself, reducing you to the role of 'order taker.' Your job is crucial to the sale in a couple of key areas. First, you face competition from other similar products, other companies, the other demands on the customer's budget, and inertia. Sometimes, the toughest competition is the customer's desire to keep doing what they are already doing. By identifying the customer's problems and mindset upfront, you'll be able to accurately gauge just where your competition lies and put together a plan to properly present your solution as the appropriate choice.

**Assume the Meeting**

You may have heard the old saying advising you to always "assume the sale." It's good advice and it's something you should be doing when looking to get that sales appointment. Assume that your solution is going to be of value to every customer until you find otherwise. Sure, there are times when you'll have to admit that there isn't a fit for your product with a certain customer, but wait until you get farther into the process before you make that determination.

For instance, offer two different times of meeting as a choice instead of asking if a meeting would be okay. Tell them that you'll be in the area tomorrow and ask what coffee you could bring. All of these types of questions assume the appointment and stand a good chance of getting agreement.

That type of confidence will help in getting an appointment with most anyone who has an interest in what you're selling. But you can also use persuasion principles here to put the odds of getting that first meeting in your favor.

Let's take a look at each and how they could be used to land that important first meeting.

### Reciprocity

Here is a good time to break out a freebie from your prepared stash that must be hand delivered. "I have a great free system on developing a call handling system for your company. I could drop by and walk you through it tomorrow or would Wednesday be better?" "I can get some information together on what we have to offer. I can drop it off and bring pizza for lunch tomorrow or would Friday be better?"

### Scarcity

You should always have an 'opportunity window' that gives you an immediacy to get an appointment. This limited timeframe uses Scarcity to help persuade your prospect to agree to a meeting before he or she loses access to something. "I have just a few models remaining that I think would be perfect for you. I'll stop by tomorrow and see what would work best." "We have a special pricing voucher available through the end of the month. I can stop by tomorrow to drop one off and talk a little more about what needs you have right now."

### Authority

Setting yourself as an expert during this first call can be helpful later on. It's an ideal point to invite someone to one of your events. "I'm doing a new product orientation for some clients tomorrow. Let me buy you lunch, and then you can sit in and see how our program works." "I'll be speaking at a small business meeting on Friday. Stop by, and I'll go over more details with you afterward. I'll text you the address and time now."

### Consistency

If you've already started the call off with a question that got a positive response, you've already set yourself up for Consistency. But there are other ways to use Consistency to get that appointment. The best is to appeal to what is consistent with the prospect's view of who they are. "Most of the folks on your street are using us to keep their lawns looking great. What time tomorrow would be good to show you how you can use our services?" "Most companies who are as busy as yours can save quite a bit with our program. Is tomorrow morning or afternoon better to get you some more detail on how it works?"

### Liking

Setting yourself up to use Liking can often go hand-in-hand with Reciprocity. Giving something with no expectation of something in return can often help make you likable. Also, make a point of being respectful of the person's time and schedule. Be as flexible as possible and accommodating to the needs of each prospect. And don't forget the compliments when possible! Nobody is going to make an appointment with someone they don't like.

### Consensus

Highlight anything you can to shows your dominance in some area of the industry to use Consensus. "We have repaired more roofs in your neighborhood than anyone else." "We have become the main software solution for businesses like yours." People like to be one of the packs. Show them where your pack is when you get an opportunity.

### Unity

People like to do business with someone who is "one of them." Do what you can to find some commonality with the prospect, so they are more likely to give you that appointment. Mention customers, friends, or family that you have living near them. Point out that you or a family member used to work for a company just like theirs or in the same industry. "You're a teacher? My aunt taught high school English for 20 years." Do what you can in the short amount of time you have on that first contact to point up any similarities you have with the client to show you are on their side.

### Extra Tools to Get Your Foot in the Door

Getting that first meeting is possibly the most crucial part of your sales process. You can't make the sale if you never get to present your solutions, and you can't design solutions for your prospect if you can't get that first meeting.

So, if all else fails, here are just a few additional tips to help you make that all important first contact:

- **Ask for a 'yes.'** As we mentioned earlier, it's important to ask questions early, especially questions designed to get a 'yes.' "Are you currently trying to improve your sales force?" Who isn't? "Would you be interested in a way to cut 25 percent off your home energy bill?" You can also try qualifiers, like "Are you currently spending more than $1000 a month on vehicle expenses?" If you can't help a person who answers 'no' to that question, then you've either gotten an early 'yes' or saved yourself some time. Getting the 'yes' early here uses Consistency to keep the agreement going for the request for a meeting next.

- **Give them a reason.** It helps to let the person know exactly what you want to do during the meeting. Research has shown that people are most likely to do someone a favor if they know *why* the person needs the favor. We've mentioned several reasons above that you can use, but also don't be afraid to make it personal. If you can strike a congenial tone early in the call, ask them to help you out by giving you some more details about your business. "Even if you aren't interested, I would still like to learn more about your process so I can help out other businesses like yours."

- **Emphasize their free choice.** This may sound odd, but research has shown that when asking for a favor, people are much more likely to say 'yes' when you remind them that the choice is theirs. "I know you can choose from several companies for your phone system. I really appreciate you taking some time to meet with me." "Of course, you don't need to accept it, but I would love to bring coffee by and see what you're currently doing with your landscaping."

- **Drop by in person.** Most times, you'll be making your first contact through phone or email, but that isn't always the best way. A 2016 study showed that despite what people predicted, they were more successful asking for something of a stranger when they asked in person. You may think you seem trustworthy in your emails or phone calls, but research has found that most people are trusted more when they meet someone face-to-face.

## Developing Solutions

While we are still not at a stage where we can actively sell, we are ready to put our sale in motion. That starts with research.

As we've talked about before, you'll already be researching industry topics regularly to stay up on trends and important to your customers, setting yourself to use Authority during your sales cycle. The research we're talking about here is the specific research you'll need to do on your customer, their situation and how you will be able to best solve their problem with what you're offering.

### *Forget Pitching, Start Listening*

First, a warning; you may find enough about your customer during your first contact to find out they don't need what you have to offer. Maybe the problem they have isn't going to be solved with your product or service. Or maybe their problem isn't really big enough to spend what's needed for your solution. That's not going to be a sale you can make without coercion and that's not the kind of sale anyone likes to do. Even though you may make that sale, the client will eventually realize what happened and feel like they made a mistake, which will end up being more harmful to you in the end.

Being persuasive is not coercing or manipulating someone to do something that is not in their best interest. Persuasiveness is a means of helping someone see that you have the best solution to their problem and that you are the one to make it happen. The first step in that sale is to learn what your client's specific problems are.

### *Interviewing Your Customers*

The most valuable research you can do is to listen to your customers and prospects. They will tell you exactly what you need to know to sell to them because they know the problems that they face on a day-to-day basis in their business or their household.

You may have heard the old axiom that nobody has ever gone to buy a quarter-inch drill. What they are buying is a quarter-inch *hole*. What this means is that people only have needs and desired outcomes. In purchasing, a smart salesperson knows that emotion trumps logic every time. If a person is excited about doing something, they will ignore every logical roadblock to getting it done.

During your first meeting, you'll be listening much more than you'll be talking. That's because you are on a fact-finding mission. You need to find out why the customer agreed to talk with you, find out what their specific problems are and how they need those problems solved.

Here's where you need to ask open-ended questions and get the prospect talking. You may find more opportunities than you initially knew about. You may also find out that the customer isn't actually dealing with the problem they initially thought they were. Only by listening and probing for more information can you hope to find out how you can make a difference.

The flip side of that fact-finding is that you may find out the prospective customer doesn't need you. Maybe once you understand the problem they really have, your solution may not be the one to fix it. That's okay, too. It's better to find out now that the prospect isn't a good fit for what you have to offer and move on, instead of spending a lot of your valuable time and energy on a sale that isn't going to happen in the end.

The whole point of learning more about your customer's needs is to find out if you can help. If not, nobody's time has been wasted. You might even be able to point the customer in the right direction. Don't lose the opportunity to build Authority and Liking with the client. Stay in touch! They may need you in the future. But don't be afraid to walk away from a customer that doesn't need you. There are plenty out there who do.

You'll never know for sure if you can help your prospective customer until you find out more about their problem. That's why learning to be a great interviewer can make your sales job so much easier. A face-to-face interview is the only way to learn how someone *feels* about a problem or challenge they are facing. By taking their emotions into account, you can learn exactly what problem you need to focus on solving.

If you don't have much experience doing interviews, here are a few tips to keep in mind to get the most out of that first meeting:

- **Realize that you are there to listen, not sell.** Nobody wants to hear from you. They want to hear about themselves, and by association, how you can help them. Make this first contact about letting the prospect talk, and when they stop, find the quickest way to get them talking again.

- **Don't ask yes-no questions.** Asking someone for an answer that can be handled as a 'yes' or 'no' fails for two reasons. First, it's easy to answer quickly and doesn't prompt your customer to give you any details. Secondly, you are inserting your opinion and getting the other person to agree or disagree, which doesn't tell you anything you don't already know. "Do you currently have problems with your sales team?" doesn't help you nearly as much as "Tell me about your top problems with your salespeople." By asking this type of open-ended question, you will often find out something you didn't even think of.

- **Learn to prompt.** In the example above, suppose you get the answer, "The team spends more time in the office than they do with clients." Instead of accepting that as the answer, you might follow up with, "How do you feel they should spend their time?" This deepens the answer and gets them talking more. Each answer to an open-ended question should suggest other threads that you can pull at to broaden your understanding of the customer's needs.

- **Pay attention.** It may seem simple, but many people develop a bad habit during an interview of thinking about their next question instead of listening to the answer. The only way you are going to find out what question to ask next is to listen to the answers you get.

- **Use notes, but don't interview from them.** Having written notes can help you make sure you cover all the bases, but many people will use them as a crutch, so they don't need to pay attention to the person they are talking to. Have you ever had a conversation with someone who won't look at you, and looks at everything else in the room but you? How annoying is that? Don't do it to your customer. Instead, keep a short list to look at toward the end of your discussion. When you check it, see if you feel you could answer all of the questions you have written down based on what you just learned. If there are still areas you are unsure of, ask for clarification then before you wrap up.

## Assessing Needs

Once you have identified the customer's problem, you can work to help them fix it. That's why the most successful salespeople are problem solvers.

Everyone has a problem that needs to be solved. Consumers and businesses alike are dealing with problems every day. Individuals have repairs that need to be made, financial worries that need to be solved, housing that needs to be altered or changed to meet the needs and wants of their family, necessities that need to be bought within their budget.

Businesses are built to deal with and solve those individual problems. You may be selling something that helps an individual to solve a problem directly or you may be selling solutions for businesses so that they can more effectively solve those problems for their customers, but sales are always about one thing: effectively and efficiently eliminating a problem.

In addition to finding out more about the prospect's problems, you should also be assessing how they are thinking about their challenges as well. While finding out the true nature of your prospect's problem is probably the most important in knowing what solution you should offer, assessing your customer's mindset is arguably the most important effort you can make to find out *how* to present your solution to that problem later.

Once you have conducted your interview with your customer, jot down some quick notes regarding the problems you heard about that you believe you can solve. You don't want to take a long time to do this, but you do want to get down the information while it's still fresh in your mind. As you're doing this, it's a good idea to recap a bit for the customer. "It sounds like you would really like to solve…" This lets the customer know that you were listening, and may even prompt some more information.

Now is not the time to solve those problems. What you should do is use the promise of solutions as the reason for another meeting. Who doesn't love a cliff-hanger? Just the curiosity of wanting to see the result of your work is usually enough of a draw to get the next meeting for your presentation. After recapping what you've learned from talking to them, set up the next meeting. Let them know that until your next meeting, you're going to be working on some solutions for their challenges.

What you can do before you leave is give an idea of what is possible with what you have to offer. Without giving specific answers to that customer's situation, you should talk about your products and services in general so they have a taste of what type of a solution you will be able to offer. The time between meetings will allow space for your customer to start formulating new questions and begin making the decision to buy. Giving the customer a "glimpse of the future" with your product can have them much more ready to buy when it comes time for the presentation, and you ask for the sale.

Sales great Brian Tracy also offers a few of his time-honored tips to remember during and sales meeting which also go toward the principles of persuasion. I'll relate a few of them here and show how persuasion plays a role in each.

- **Thank the client for their time.** Talking with a salesperson is often the last thing a busy person wants to do. Even if they called you initially, you still could go a long way toward establishing Liking by recognizing the time that they have granted you.

- **Let the customer know what to expect up front.** You have indirectly (or directly, depending on your approach) promised not to sell your customer when you set the appointment for this first meeting, so before the meeting starts, go over again what you want to accomplish and highlight the fact that you won't be trying to sell them anything today. You are here to listen and learn so that you can find solutions that best fit their situation. Building Reciprocity by giving your time and expertise with no expectation of an immediate decision will go a long way toward building your client's trust, earning you future goodwill.

- **Don't be afraid to offer advice.** Even though you aren't giving specific solutions regarding your products, giving the prospect an idea of your knowledge of the industry and products you have will give the client value for their time and will help to build your Authority in what you have to offer.

- **Be ready for questions.** Most clients ask the same types of questions of you once the meeting is over. Be ready to answer those inquiries directly and well. Questions like past work, experience, and other customers are bound to come up. Be ready to hit those questions out of the park.

- **Don't be afraid to sell yourself.** It may not be the best time to sell your products, but this is the perfect time to sell your experience and expertise. Building your Authority will help with persuasion later, but it also allows you to show the added value that you provide with your expertise.

## Debriefing Yourself

Immediately after your meeting, you need to stop and gather your thoughts on paper or in a digital document. This debriefing of yourself is important to do as quickly as possible because you don't want fine points and emotions of the meeting to slip away. Don't worry about structure or format. Instead, put down everything you just learned about this customer and their needs. If you have had a productive meeting, the customer should have told you everything you need to know about their top concerns.

We also noted earlier that you needed to be watching for clues on *how* the customer was thinking about their problems. While you're putting down each of the points you noticed during your interview meeting, note anything that the customer said about those particular problems that stuck out in your mind.

These types of statements are usually indicative of how they *feel* about that problem. These feelings we can term *emotional motivators*. Emotions are, by far, the biggest driving force behind most decisions people make, regardless of how logical people believe they are. According to research, humans may not be able to make a decision effectively without emotions.

### *Emotions in the Buying Process*

Neurologist Dr. Antonio Damasio wrote in his book *Descartes' Error: Emotion, Reason, and the Human Brain* that research found patients who had suffered prefrontal cortical damage were unable to make even simple choices. Because of their injury, these people were physically unable to create emotions, and this was found to greatly limit their ability to make even simple choices like which color socks to wear.

This emotional decision making is particularly important where value decisions come into play, such as deciding on the best choice between two similar offerings. When your prospect weighs what you're offering versus the competition, you better believe that emotion could be the deciding factor in the choice they make. Even self-improvement and sales wizard Dale Carnegie noted the importance of the client's feelings in the sales process, once writing, "When dealing with people, remember you are not dealing with creatures of logic, but with creatures of emotion."

Buying emotions can cover a wide range, but here are a few general areas of interest when it comes to selling:

- **Status** - Those interested in status are going to be looking to set themselves apart from the rest of their friends, neighbors, or other businesses in their field. Business clues from your interview would include discussion of what their competition often does or talk about how hard they have worked to become number one in an industry. For consumers, look for clues in how they describe what they want in terms of what their friends did in a similar situation or what they have noticed when visiting their neighbors.

- **Convenience -** Everybody wants to achieve more, be more productive, and do it easily without changing much of their schedule. The on-demand, get-anything-easily world of the Internet has prompted this type of thinking for nearly everything we purchase now. Note if your client talked a lot about productivity, difficulties in other systems they've looked at, or constant discussions of their personal time.

- **Reassurance -** Nobody wants to make a mistake. In the early days of business computing, there was a popular saying: "Nobody ever got fired for recommending IBM." The company had become so dominant in the industry that no one wanted to risk their career on choosing a competitor. If you noticed mentions of needing help in a certain area, looking for an expert in something or questions about experience, this tells you that this customer highly values reassurance.

## Productizing your Offerings

In this example, you would have several ways to address this customer's concerns. You could simply repair the siding that is damaged, but you know they already don't like the siding overall. You could replace all of the sidings with something of better quality, but you have several choices available here. Plus, many customers have opted for additional services, such as an additional layer of insulation under the siding, changing or painting the soffits, putting up new eve spouts, and more.

Here's where you are going to need pre-choose a few best options and package them into neat "products" that can be easily selected. You may want to limit your choices to the top two or three options. The reason for this is that people don't make decisions well. Most suffer what is called "decision paralysis" when faced with too many choices.

In one study, 300 doctors were presented with a patient with a hip problem. They were told that the patient had exhausted all non-surgical treatments, and all of the doctors recommended a surgical hip replacement. Easy choice.

Then, groups of these doctors were given a new decision. Right before surgery, the doctors were told a new medicine had been found that might be beneficial. When the first group of doctors was told that only one new medicine had been found, most of the doctors canceled the surgery and recommended trying the new medicine. That again seems straightforward enough.

The interesting part was the group of doctors that were told that *two* new medicines had been found that might be effective. In that group, most of the doctors *still chose surgery*. When faced with too many choices, even these experts went with the default option, which was to continue with the surgery. In your case, as a salesperson, the default option is no sale. To make sure you make the sale instead of causing indecision, make the choice simple.

With your plan firmly put together, it's time to put together your presentation and make the sale.

# Chapter 4:
## Killing the Presentation

The presentation is where you make the ask, looking to sum everything up into a couple of easy choices that answer all of the questions and pain points for the customer to make the decision to buy easy.

### It's Not Logical; It's Emotional

As we've talked about in the previous section, buying is an emotional choice as much or even more than a logical one. So, as you build your sales presentation, don't forget to add the emotion. The notes you made after that first contact meeting are going to be your outline for the emotions to address during your next meeting.

Why are emotions so important? Because emotions act as a type of "shorthand" for the brain. According to behavior experts, emotional reactions are 3,000 times faster than rational thoughts in the brain. Sensory input is processed five times faster than rational thoughts by the emotional parts of the brain. And, most importantly for influence on making decisions, persuasiveness is as much as 24 times more effective with emotional rather than rational appeals.

In their book *Switch,* Chip and Dan Heath reduced the brain's function to a simple metaphor of an elephant, a rider and a path. The rider is logical reasoning, and the path is representational of the environment where a decision is made. The elephant? You guessed it; it's emotion. While you can reason with the rider and try and control the path to your best ability, that elephant will run away with your presentation if you have planned for it ahead of time.

To make sure your presentation covers all the bases, make sure you use emotions along with the reason in your pitch. Here are some easy ways to include an emotional punch in your presentation:

- **Tell a story.** To make your points more memorable, consider tying key facts to a short story that drives the point home. You can tell a story to illustrate your solution to their problem or highlight the main idea in what would otherwise be an overwhelming sea of facts. Personal stories can make the solution seem real, and make the idea lock-in as an obvious scenario.

- **Visualize statistics.** If your presentation depends on statistics in a large way, packaging those numbers up in charts and graphs can make it much faster and easier for your customers to grab that information and hold onto it. Also, try to tie the numbers to an emotional meaning. For instance, a 7 percent reduction in downtime might not mean much, but increasing revenue by $27 thousand per year means increased financial security and means more to the client.

- **Make it personal.** When you talk about what your product can do, don't talk only about testing and industry sales figures. Instead, find ways to make that performance relate personally to the person you're talking to. Take our home siding example from earlier. Instead of just saying that the siding you're recommending is the best looking in the market, but talk about how much they'll enjoy their back deck and yard with this beautiful new siding across the back of their house. Show how beautiful it will be with the existing wood tones of the deck. Make them see in their mind how happy they will be with that purchase.

- **Use metaphors when possible.** There are only so many facts that a brain can hold. Using metaphors helps turn that dry information into a picture that the brain can hold onto much easier. When talking about the increased volume of an industrial pump, don't just talk about the increased flow rate, but say something like, "Next to your current pumps, this capacity is like a fire hose against your lawn sprinkler." That picture makes more of an impact on the listener than any percentages you could offer.

### Emotions and the Principles of Persuasion

Emotions are a large part of the principles of persuasion as well. Here's a brief idea of how various emotions are at play in each of the seven principles and what you can do in your presentation to take advantage of these ideas to make your pitch work toward the sale.

### *Reciprocity*

You've already set up Reciprocity in your earlier contact by giving your prospects something of value. That receiving plays into a customer's emotions by making then more likely to help you out in return. So during your presentation, reference one of the resources you gave them earlier or the lunch you provided. It shouldn't be over (good persuasion never is), but you could say something like, "If you remember when I brought lunch over, you told me how you were hoping to get your revenues up by 10 percent this year." Just this gentle reference will help to call back the reciprocity you're hoping to be able to use during your sales presentation.

### *Scarcity*

People have a great fear of loss. Research shows that people react much more reliably to fear than reward. The fear of loss is one of those basic fears that everyone reacts to. Scarcity refers to this fear of loss and shows how what you're offering is limited; deciding to take advantage of what you're selling *now* is important, so the customer doesn't lose out. Find ways to make your product or time frame seem like a reason to make a decision now.

### *Authority*

You have also been building authority throughout the appointment-setting process and your first meeting. By selling yourself and your expertise throughout this time you've built authority for yourself. People are much more likely to follow the suggestions of someone they feel is an authority figure. One interesting experiment had researchers ask strangers for change for the parking meter. One group wore normal street clothes, while the other wore a uniform. People were much more likely to give a change to the person in the uniform because they respected the authority this gave him. Dressing the part of an accomplished person in your field will help you also.

Also, if you haven't done it already, highlight the accomplishments and experience of your company in your presentation. Adding this additional authority will help to build your persuasive pitch.

### *Consistency*

People all have a view of themselves, a story of what they would do in any circumstance that they will try to protect. If they find that people like them do a certain thing or believe a certain way, they will subconsciously begin to do things that agree with that picture. If you point up how much they have already told you about their situation and how much work you have done on this together so far, they will naturally want to continue to bring this project to an end and make the purchase. Use opportunities during your presentation to show how the customer has already participated in a lot of what you have come up with as a solution, and it will make them feel that the purchase is just the next logical step.

### *Liking*

Starting every meeting with a little small talk and a little flattery where appropriate doesn't just work on a date. It will work in most any personal situation and it can work in your favor when persuading someone that you have the best solution to their problem. If the prospect likes you, they will want to help you accomplish your goal of making the sale.

### *Consensus*

People want to belong and be part of the group. From an emotional standpoint, making your customer feel like part of the club can help you in convincing them to become customers. Giving them special "internal" data, a few company promotional items like a shirt or mug or even a 'thank you' email from your boss thanking them for allowing you to visit will make your prospect feel like they are already on the "inside" of your company, and they'll want to do what it takes to stay part of the group.

## *Unity*

The newest "official" persuasion principle is a must for salespeople. Often referred to as "selling from the customer's side of the table," working as the customer's advocate as opposed to a salesperson shows that you are on their side and people will buy from those they feel are "one of them." Instead of putting your presentation together to sell something to your customer, put things together in a way that shows you are helping them get the best solution from your company. Pointing up things you did for them, such as asking for special pricing or a custom package to accomplish their goals "for" them will show that you and the customer are on the same team.

## Pre-Planning for Objection

We would all like to think that our sales presentations will go off without a hitch. "No, please, put the check away until I've finished going over the package!"

Then the alarm goes off, and you wake up.

There will be problems, questions, and concerns that will come up during your presentation and you will be able to handle them confidently and quickly if you've done some pre-planning.

Handling objection is the main part of any sales professional's job, so to make your sales presentation effective, let's look at some methods for using persuasion to help turn things back in your favor when you hit a bump in your presentation.

## *The LAER Model*

To effectively handle objections in the sales process, it's necessary to look at the selling cycle as a relationship between you and the buyer. No relationships go perfectly at all times. Different people have different views and different backgrounds, so it's no surprise that you might see something like a no-brainer while your prospect sees it as a no-deal.

One framework that helps to keep this relationship on track is something called the LAER method. Sales training organization Carew International developed this method in their *Dimensions of Professional Selling* training program as a way of dealing with objections during the sales process. We'll use LAER again when it comes time to make the final negotiation, but in this context, here's how we will use the LAER framework to deal with objections.

LAER (pronounced "LAYER") is a method for dealing with the objection which stands for Listen, Acknowledge, Explore, and Respond. To be ready to use this framework as a way to plan for objection, let's first go over how to utilize each step in your objection response.

<u>Listen</u>

Here we are telling you to listen again. You may be getting the idea that this is a very important skill, and it is. During your presentation, just as you did during your first meeting, pay attention to what your customer is saying. You'll be doing far more talking during this meeting, but when the client talks, make sure you understand what they are telling you and deal with it as it happens as much as possible.

Don't just start talking from a script you've used a million times. Instead, your presentation should offer natural points where you can get feedback, so you know if you need to adjust. When objections go on unsaid or ignored, they will greatly detract from your message.

<u>Acknowledge</u>

To make sure you were listening and to show your customer that you were paying attention, ask for clarification if needed or simply rephrase and repeat what the customer has said, so they understand you were listening. Don't simply answer, be thoughtful and make sure you have time to properly put together your response. Taking some extra time to respond is important so that you don't look flustered or caught off guard. Maintaining our Authority throughout the presentation is important.

## Explore

Before you answer, try to explore the objection a little further. Ask for more details or specifics. Again, you are looking to gain as much information before you need to respond with your counter to their objection. By asking for more complete details, you reduce the question from a mere rock thrown at your pretty presentation, changing it into valuable input. Treat the question as though finding out more information will make your answer the best it can be, and help the client in the process. This extra time out can also help to diffuse the situation if the client is upset by something or it can help to make what may seem like a mountain into more of a simple molehill.

## Respond

After taking time to explore the question, it's then time to respond. In the next chapter, we'll deal with some of the more common objections and how to respond to them appropriately using this LAER method. For now, plan space in your presentation for these moments and remember not to steamroll past them or fail to give them the proper attention. By building in a little extra time to your presentation, you'll be able to effectively handle these moments as they come up.

Don't be surprised if the client doesn't talk at all during the presentation. If that happens, you may want to have some pre-designed questions for them that can be answered affirmatively. That helps to keep them interested and focus and continues building on the Consistency principle that is important to closing the sale, getting that final all-important "yes."

## *Common Questions*

The other part of your presentation that you should plan for is questions about you and your company. You should try and work the answers to these questions into your presentation as early as possible to that your prospect will be put at ease that you knocked out some of his or her questions without needing to ask them.

As you do more and more presentations, you'll quickly begin to get your list of questions that you get asked about your specific product or company. If you've already had some experience, think back to your last several presentations and jot down the questions that you've heard most often, especially those you found hard to answer. Add answers to these questions into your basic presentation template, so you don't forget to touch on them every time.

If you need some help or you're new to sales, these common questions will get you started.

- **Why should I choose you?** Okay, I'll start with the most tired question. I feel like this question is more of a stall than anything and if you get this one, the customer may be halfway to sending you to the curb anyway. Didn't I just show you what we can do together? But seriously, if you do get this question, treat it with respect and have a killer answer ready. Focus on the unique value of your offering; the longevity of you, the company or both; or past projects that you are proud of, whether you were involved or not. You need to make this look like the most obvious choice imaginable.

- **What makes you different?** This question can be an opportunity for you to brag on your customer service, past projects, or outstanding people. What you should avoid doing is talking about the competition. Sure, this question invites you to trash your competitors, but don't take the bait. If you want to contrast your company, do it in positive terms. Instead of saying something like, "If you ever call Company X, make sure you have some time to kill," contrast from the other direction. "We make it a priority to have one of the fastest call response times in the market, beating our competitors consistently in outside testing." Accentuating your positive will naturally call into question the competitor's negatives without making you sound petty.

- **What do I do if I change my mind?** Your response here will rely entirely on your company, so find out what the procedure is. If your policy is no returns, no refunds then state that in the positive. "We have a satisfaction rate over 99 percent, and if you aren't happy for any reason, we'll work to make it right, whatever it takes." If you have a company case of something you did to the extreme to fix a problem, you may want to have that story at the ready, if needed.

### Learn What the Competition Says

Another common thing that you should address in your presentation is anything you know that the competition says about you or your company. Don't shy away from this type of trash talk. If you aren't winning, nobody talks about you. It's better that *everybody* is talking about you. Just be prepared to deal with what they're saying, preferably by putting something to squash the questions before they come up.

The competition will also have some favorite selling points that you can bet will be used during their presentation. While these aren't pointed at you directly, they are meant to differentiate them from the competition, and that's you.

Here are some easy ways to do a little recon on your competition so you can counteract their sales tactics in your presentation.

- **Track the competition's advertising.** Visit their website often so you get tracked by their online advertising, and make sure you look through all the junk mail you can get your hands on to see if they have any direct mail happening. Determining how your customers found out about you can also tell you where to look for your competition as well. If they saw them on TV or heard them on radio, sample popular stations once in awhile to see if you can catch their ads. Note their points and address the same points in your presentations.

- **Visit their locations or websites.** Act as a customer. Unless their staff knows you, you can even go through the early stages of their sales process. This will give you a lot of info on how they work with customers and give a lot of ideas on how to differentiate yourself during your presentation. If you can't do it yourself, talk to customers after they sign up with you, and have them tell stories of what it was like to work with the other guys.

- **Network with industry friends.** Make contacts with people in businesses that have connections to your competitors, and ask them occasionally if they know what's happening over at Company X. Often, these stories will just come up if you hang out with the right people on occasion.

- **Get on the mailing list.** If your competitor has an email list or customer program that gets sent advertising specials, sign up! This is the easiest way to get information sent directly to your email or mailbox.

# Chapter 5:
## Negotiating the Deal

Are you enjoying the book so far? If so, we would really appreciate if you could take a moment to leave a short review on Amazon, it really helps us!

Your presentation went off without a hitch and now you're ready to pick up that signature and check when the customer wants to "think about it." Something is holding them back from pulling the trigger, but what is it. Price? Problems with your product? While you still have momentum going, it's time to start negotiating to try and address the problems standing in your way and keep your deal moving toward completion.

### Evaluating Your Options

Any time a salesperson reaches a sticking point in a deal, panic can seep into their mind and sabotage the negotiations. Once you allow the customer to make you worry you're not going to close, the customer starts running the negotiation and can put you in a bad place from a strategic point of view.

If you have built goodwill through Reciprocity and Liking throughout the sales process up to this point, you should be in good shape. Even so, it's difficult to tell yourself that when you're watching your deal go up in smoke. What should you do?

First, relax. This step is always expected, and by doing a little pre-planning, you can make sure that you are as ready as possible when push-back rears its ugly head. So take a deep breath and assess your position.

In negotiation, you should always have your Best Alternative to a Negotiated Agreement (BATNA) in mind before the negotiation ever starts. Negotiation experts recommend knowing what your "walk away" point is in any negotiation, and that's what your BATNA is. Your customer also has its own BATNA, whether they realize it or not. You need to know both if you want to come out with everybody happy.

The best option, of course, is not to *need* the sale. The best defense for this is to have several deals in the pipeline at any one time, so losing one isn't a death sentence. If this isn't possible and if you have some discretion over pricing, decide where your bottom line needs to be to make sense even to do the deal. Maybe you can strip down features or get the customer into a lower rung service contract to start. You'll win their confidence and upgrade them over the long haul.

What other options do you have? Have these at the ready before the sales presentation even begins. Does your company offer staggered pay arrangements? Financing deals? Lesser priced options? Discounts for upfront payment? Find out your options and keep up-to-date on any programs your company can offer to get someone on board. Keep these in your back pocket, but never lead with them. And don't be in a hurry to use them either. Always do everything you can to find a way to negotiate with persuasion before giving in to the other side. This way, you know you always have fall back positions.

**Dealing with Objection**

Into every sales presentation, a little objection must fall. We all wish that every sales presentation would move smoothly from offer to sale. Unfortunately, it rarely works that way. Since you know that objections will undoubtedly occur, plan now to have ways to answer your most common objections. When you hit a snag, you'll be ready to handle it head-on.

To give us a set of objection power tools, we can once again use the principles of persuasion to help us find our way through the problem to reach that final sale.

### *How Persuasion Figures into Objection*

The principles of persuasion can be of great help in negotiating the final close. We have been talking about laying a foundation for persuasion throughout your process when you weren't asking for the sale. Now that you're ready to close, it's time to cash in on everything you've been investing in persuasion up to this point, as well as using the principles in some new ways. Let's take a look at the seven principles, and see how we can use them to advantage in negotiation.

<u>Reciprocity</u>

Negotiating involves some give and take and the best way to get cooperation is to give some first. Try offering some additional value right out of the box, something that doesn't cost anything or doesn't take anything out of the budget. "Normally, our setup is an additional fee, but let me handle that for you myself and save you the fee." Once you've given them something, they are now in need of giving you something in return.

Another strategy that has been found to work involving reciprocity can be to set up your "giving" by asking for a larger sale first. Research has found that if you ask for something smaller right after being turned down for the larger ask, you tend to be successful more often than starting with the smaller proposition. By giving in quickly and making your prospect feel bad for turning you down, they are more likely to give you the approval of the smaller ask in return.

## Scarcity

Scarcity is always the go-to tactic when it comes to the "I want to think it over" stall. "I need to get you in as soon as possible to get this price" is something all salespeople have used from time to time. But are there less obvious ways to use Scarcity?

Looking at the above example, where we opened with a ridiculously big ask to set up the smaller one, use that failed ask in another way. "Call the office" to try and get a better deal on the failed offer, only to "find out" that it's no longer available. Get a "special hold" on the smaller ask for a limited time in response and see if this moves the needle. Be careful with this, because if you put a deadline in place and the buyer waits you out, you've taken yourself out of the negotiation.

## Authority

Authority can be used for reassurance. If you've been selling from your customer's side of the table, you can use this partnership to assure them you don't have anything better to offer. You can also assure them that knowing what you know after you've been in the company this long, you would take the deal the way you have it set up to get the best value. Let them know that they are "free to do whatever they want" (remembering our earlier technique) but that this deal is the best way to purchase.

You can also use a battle with Authority to set up a "good cop, bad cop" scenario as we described above. A call to your hard-line boss doesn't go well, but you use your Authority to personally approve a deal and "take the consequences" to get the customer on board.

<u>Consistency</u>

You've been working at getting your prospect to give you small agreements throughout the initial sales cycle and you want to keep that moving your way now. Finding small things to agree on while moving toward your final goal will help eventually to make the ultimate 'yes' happen.

In that area, another negotiation tactic that has been backed up by research is nothing more than restating all of the areas of the agreement you already have in the current offer. Experts at Harvard's Program on Negotiation point out that the most common mistake negotiators tend to make is to draw a "line in the sand" over the areas where they differ when in most cases they already have agreed on several points.

Highlight the points where you already have an agreement, and then work on what needs to be negotiated. The other side is much more likely to give more after they see how close you already are to each other.

<u>Liking</u>

Always make sure you start the negotiation by acknowledging the other person's objection. Your clients will like you much better if you validate their concerns and offer a remedy that should satisfy them. No one wants to feel like their opinion doesn't hold water, and simply restating their concerns as valid will keep them from being quite as defensive. Keeping your likability can only help you finally finish the sale and play well for you down the road.

### Consensus

Don't be afraid to bring up your experience with other customers who are just like this one and let them know that your offer is quite common with all of them. "I realize you don't feel you need the additional labor, but my customers often decide after the fact that they wish they had done the extra prep. Adding it on afterward is much more expensive, so my customers who opt to add this in from the beginning are much happier with the outcome." Using other terms like "most popular package" or "our standard system" will give them a feeling of Consensus as well.

### Unity

Reminding your customers that you are going to be their point of contact long after the sale shows that you are on their side. Why would you give them a deal that they won't be happy with if it's only going to give you an upset client to deal with going forward? Tell them again that you are here to give them the best experience possible throughout the purchase cycle, which includes after the sale. This is why you are recommending the offer you have.

## *Most Common Forms of Objection*

We talked earlier about how the LAER model (Listen, Acknowledge, Explore, Respond) can help to overcome objections during a sales presentation. Now that we've gone through how the seven principles of persuasion can help to push through objections, let's look at some of the most common forms of objection and how we can use the techniques of persuasion coupled with the LAER method to climb past those roadblocks.

### Common Objection #1: Price

It's always about the money. If you have been in sales for any amount of time, you know that the best presentations can have the wheels fly off when it comes time to write the check. Since this is such a common objection, it's good to have some remedies in your back pocket to get past this hurdle.

You may hear, "This is just too expensive." Using the LAER method, acknowledge what they have said, and explore their price concern a bit more. Expensive compared to what? Are you comparing my price to a competitor? If so, respond by breaking your cost down into smaller line items to show the number of goods or services they are receiving for each part of the price. Often these smaller numbers feel much more attainable than the total.

Are you comparing my price to doing nothing? Then respond by highlighting the savings you are providing, the costs in their existing budget that you are replacing, or the costs that they will likely incur without your solution. The customer has a need of some kind, or they wouldn't have agreed to talk to you. We spoke earlier of the need to know the customer's BATNA (Best Alternative to a Negotiated Settlement). That BATNA is what they will have if they do nothing, or keep doing what they are already doing. Know the cost of that BATNA before you go into your presentation, and you'll have the perfect response ready for objections about the price.

### Common Objection #2: Inertia

People don't like to change. The risk of the unknown is often a greater fear than the risk of slowly losing what they already may have. People like to keep the status quo. But again, the customer recognized some problem or they wouldn't have talked to you in the first place. Once you've listened to their objection, acknowledge that "cold feet" are common before making a change. Explore their concerns further. Is the fear actually related to cost, to lose what they have, or to a part of your offer that they don't understand? Once you've clarified the actual basis for the fear, you need to reassure them that nobody likes change, but as Will Rogers once said, "Even if you are on the right track, you'll get run over if you just sit there."

Things are constantly changing and you can start to handle this objection by simply pointing out all the ways in which things have changed since they started doing things the way they do now or since they bought the thing your solution is replacing. Change is a natural and valuable part of life, and you need to show them that this purchase is just a normal part of the progression of change.

More to the point of the Will Rogers quote above, you may be able to highlight the cost of continuing with the status quo. New products are engineered for better energy usage, lower maintenance, and easier repairs all of which save the customer money in the long run. Many services eliminate the need to add or train staff, lessen customer callbacks, and keep costly damage from happening later. These are real costs that you can contrast against the price of the service you are offering.

## Common Objection #3: Timing

"This sounds great, but I am just swamped right now. Let's do this in a few months." This is a common objection, but using the LAER framework, it's one that you can get past. Once you've listened to their concern, you can acknowledge their problem by sympathizing. "I know, so many of my customers are just running crazy." Then explore a bit just what is causing the time crunch. Once you have a more detailed idea of why their schedule is a mess right now, you'll be able to formulate your response to highlight how you are going to take care of everything, so you aren't adding to their plate. It's like they're getting your assistance in taking a problem off their plate for free! When someone is really busy, what's better than getting some extra help?

Most times, people that are busy right now are still going to be just as busy in the future. Waiting is only going to make the problem they called you about get worse. Reiterate your experience in doing just what you're offering to do for them, and detail how you will be managing the entire process, so there is nothing to add to their already long to-do list.

Common Objection #4: Another Opinion

You think you are talking to the decision maker for this sale, only to get to the point of signing the contract and finding out that they need to "run this by some other people." This is a frustrating stall in the process that can sometimes be legitimate, but often is just another example of cold feet. The key is to greet this with a smile and assume the best. Acknowledge that this is a big decision and you understand wanting to get some other input.

Exploring is a very important step in this objection because the outside input could be needed for any number of reasons. Take the time to question and find out what exactly they need from the other person they're conferring with before saying "yes." Do they need someone to sign off on the money? Will this purchase impact someone else who will want to be in the loop? Are they looking for backup from someone they feel is more knowledgeable in the subject?

Once you get clarification as to why the outside help is needed, offer more information or clarification on your part if possible to make them feel as if you have already answered the questions they have. If possible, stress the fact that they can certainly cancel later if the other person doesn't agree with the purchase. People rarely cancel after committing, because Consistency rears its head and demands that they keep their commitments.

If you absolutely can't get past needing outside input, at least work to keep control of the process. "I understand what you're saying. What would be a good time to set down with both of you and answer all of their questions as well?" Schedule a time to meet with the other person and your client together or set a conference call. If possible, call the other person right then and put the whole issue to bed quickly. Make sure you offer your assistance in explaining things to the other person, and you'll make sure you can at least not let things get off track when you aren't around.

**Assume the Sale**

While these aren't all of the objections you'll run into, you should be able to use these examples as a template for how to design your objection handling in common situations you run into in your specific process. Modeling your responses using the LAER framework will help you to quickly and easily design responses to objections and keep your sale moving toward the finish line.

Above all, the well-worn saying of "assume the sale" is never more valuable than during the final negotiation. It sometimes helps to look at the sales process as a ski slope that starts at the top of the mountain, with many obstacles and dangers between the start and the finish at the bottom of the hill. When you're at the top, you know one thing for certain: Gravity will make sure that you get to the bottom, one way or the other. Your job in navigating the hill is to recognize each obstacle in your way and make the best path around it to get to the bottom smoothly. You may need to work at it, but somehow you know that you will get to the finish.

The sales process should always be the same way in your mind. When you start the negotiation, always assume that you are going to close. It's only a matter of how, and when. Always keep moving forward, calmly deal with the obstacles you meet with confidence, and eventually your momentum will carry you naturally to the end.

With each hurdle you negotiate along the way, never forget to always ask again for the sale. We can get so wrapped up in the process sometimes that we actually forget why we came to the mountain in the first place. Each new obstacle should be looked at as simply one more opportunity to close that sale, so ask again for the customer's commitment each time you successfully navigate a problem or concern for them.

And timing is often important. Studies have shown that people are often more persuasive after someone has thanked them. So, right after the client thanks you for going through the details of their objection and working them through the problems, accept their thanks and respond with your ask. They are more likely to say "yes" at that point, so don't waste the opportunity!

# Chapter 6:
## Closing and Reselling

The close and after-close part of the sales cycle is probably the most often neglected parts of the sales cycle, but they shouldn't be. Sales are, as many things are in business, all about momentum. By putting effort into signing the deal and working with the customer after the sale is completed, you will use your success as a slingshot to propel you into the next prospects with enough energy to keep your cycle going with much less effort.

The opposite is true as well. Let the wind drop out of your sails (pun intended) at the end of the sales cycle with one customer will only make it that much harder to propel yourself into the next opportunity.

The principles of persuasion and selling psychology are still useful tools at this stage, and we'll show you how to use them to turn this sale into many more.

### Building Your Customer Relationships

The close of the sale isn't the end of the process. It's the beginning of a relationship between you and your buyer.

You are now the most important person in your company from the viewpoint of your customer and you have a lot to live up to. Like any valuable relationship, it's your responsibility to make sure you put in the effort to make sure it doesn't go sour.

What's in it for you? After all, you got what you came for, right? The sale is completed, and now your customer is a user and not a prospect. But they could be the rocket fuel that launches you into your next sale, and that is worth the effort.

Most people who purchase something feel that they have done the salesperson a favor. While you may have many, many sales that you are responsible for completing, your customer is only concerned with *one* sale; and that sale is the most important thing in the world to them. To make sure that they feel that they received the value that they were expecting from that purchase, you need to stay involved to make sure that the customer doesn't feel as if you took the money and ran.

This relationship requires you to keep your hands on the delivery and sales follow through, even if it isn't technically your job. The reason is that every relationship has value. A good relationship is a business asset like any other. We can invest in a relationship, we can build it, and when we need to, we can borrow from it. A good business relationship is a valuable thing to have and can multiply exponentially over time.

### *Personalize Delivery*

To help build your relationship with your new customer, remember that the principle of Reciprocity goes both ways. Since your customer feels that they have done something for you, they will be expecting you to help them to get the most from their new purchase. If they have a bad experience with your delivery people or your onboarding staff, they will see that as a failure of yours. In some of the ideas for getting past objections, we suggested that you reassure the customer that you would be there after the sale to make sure everything went smoothly, so now it's time to put your money where your mouth is.

Personalizing the delivery for your customer means that you need to follow up to make sure you answer any questions, provide inside help and guidance, and otherwise build your Authority and Liking persuasion tools while the customer is excited about your project. A personalized note of thanks is always appreciated, and in-person stops to make sure everybody involved with the purchase remembers you and sees your commitment can pay dividends in the future.

## *Lifetime Value*

When it comes to putting a value on your work after the sale, you should look first at the lifetime value of that customer to you and your company. Replacement sales, add-on sales after the fact, repair and service down the road, and recommendations to their friends and colleagues are just some of the ways a customer can continue to be a source of revenue for you and your company.

Also, good customer relationships can be the source of ongoing knowledge and intelligence regarding your industry, your market, and your competitors. We talked earlier how important it was to your sales presentation to be able to anticipate problems you may encounter by gathering intelligence about your competition. Your new customer will continue to be pitched by your competitors in the market, even after they complete a sale with you. Staying in regular contact with your customers after the sale and solidifying your Unity with them will earn you 'inside' information from the contacts your competition makes with your customer and will help you to close other sales.

### *Take Advantage of the Feedback Loop*

Current customers can also be a valuable source of feedback on what is working in your own sales process, and what you could improve on. You might want to do this with an email form, or if you can, schedule a time to stop by for an in-person 'debriefing' after the product is received or service begins.

Many salespeople don't like to ask for feedback, because they fear the negative. On the contrary, what you should fear is *not* hearing the negative. Finding out what areas you could improve on regarding your sales system is valuable free coaching that most professionals are willing to pay a lot of money for! Don't shy away from getting input. If you don't know what's wrong, you can't fix it, and there is always room for improvement. When it comes to sales, the sports saying of "they don't count how; they count how many" could be your eventual undoing. Bad systems have a way of compounding on themselves, eventually turning small problems that could have been corrected early into insurmountable problems that damage your ability to do business in the future.

During the on-boarding process, try to give your customer at least as much attention as you did before the sale. An occasional freebie, a lunch, a stop in just to say "hi" will go a long way toward increasing your likability, as well as the profile of your company and products.

### **Expand the Relationship**

In addition to making sure that the new purchase goes smoothly, you should also work to develop and expand your relationship with your new customer so that we can maximize their future value to the company. Now that the conversation doesn't need to be all about money, you have the opportunity to solidify your customer's loyalty to you and your company.

To expand your relationships within the customer's organization, you should use your persuasion principles to build your brand and the value of your product. Here are some areas where you can use your skills to make sure you continue to connect with your client.

### *Divide Your Time*

You need always to be developing new leads and sales prospects, selling those that are in the funnel, and closing sales that you've brought to the finish line. But when you are setting up your weekly to-do list, also don't forget to add time to service your existing clients.

Existing clients can be a great resource for all parts of your sales cycle. We talked before about asking for feedback on the sales process, but asking for feedback should be a regular part of your existing client contacts. There is no better source of information about your performance than the customers who feel comfortable with you, and they are often happy to help you with information. To foster this communication, use the principle of Reciprocity and send them information and updates regularly. A regular email newsletter is an easy way to keep current customers in the loop.

### *All the News That's Fit to Email*

Regular updates on your products and services, as well as industry and market information that you've come across, can keep your customer thinking of you. A regular email is also a great way to encourage your customers to share information as well. Include poll questions, requests for feedback on a certain story, or whatever you think might encourage participation. Interesting things you learn from this feedback can give you information to put into future newsletters and can also be a way for your customers to earn some 'bragging rights' among your clients when they celebrate a milestone or find a great use for your products.

Even personal notes about birthdays, family accomplishments, and funny stories can further solidify the Unity principle with your customers and create that "club member" atmosphere that helps you keep customers and make an inviting home for new clients.

### *Don't Forget Face Time*

Your weekly client service schedule should not only include automated things like emails. You should also set appointments for yourself, either formally or informally, to drop by your customer's location and keep your face in front of the customer. When it's time to do new business, it's often easiest to give the order to the person who is there regularly. Don't let your competition fill the void left by inattention after the sale.

Also, make it a habit to know everyone you can within the client's organization. Decisions are often made by more than one person in even the smallest of companies. If you sell direct to the consumer, don't forget the other family members. Make a habit of keeping a database of important customer information you pick up in conversations. Kids, partners, and pets should all have a place in your digital memory.

Find ways once in a while to also send out perks that the whole group can enjoy. Fruit baskets, boxes of candy, pizza for lunch, or promotional items for the whole crew are just some of the little things that go a long way to cement your ongoing relationship with your client's company.

### *Continually Add Value*

One of the best uses of your follow-up contact is to find ways to add value for your customers. In addition to the group emails we talked about above, send interesting articles as a personal email to your customer when you see something that might interest them. It doesn't even need to be industry related. A clip about their favorite sports team or restaurant can sometimes be just as interesting, and a lot more fun on days when the business isn't.

Sit down and quickly write down a list of all of the ways you can think of where you can provide value to your customers. You'll be surprised how quickly you can come up with a couple of dozen just off the top of your head. Keep that list somewhere you can easily add to it, and every time you do something your customer appreciates, add it to the list. Set a regular "tickler" appointment in your calendar to remind you when it's time to touch base with a customer again. If you're at a loss on what to do when the contact appointment pops up, glance over your list for ideas.

One key way you can add value for your clients is to help them build their network of partners and vendors. Your client is wrapped up in his or her day-to-day operation so much that they often don't get the chance to interface with other people in the industry that could be valuable for them to know. You make contact with these people all day long, so why not find ways to make introductions, or recommend other companies that you think could help out your customer? Listening for pain points that may come during conversations could give you an idea that could help their business, and build your Authority and Reciprocity in the process!

### *Thank You Says A Lot*

Above all, the one thing that goes a long way toward building the relationship with our customers is to say 'thank you' once in a while.

We all get busy, and life gets in the way. But our customers are still our customers even after the sale, and we should find a way to simply and sincerely thank them for their continued business loyalty and friendship regularly.

**Get the Referral**

Besides managing the client relationship after the sale, the other often-ignored part of the sales cycle is asking for referrals.

Referrals are the most valuable marketing you can receive. First, they are basically free. It costs almost zero marketing and advertising budget to get a referral from a customer, and yet it is the most powerful form of advertising and marketing you *can't* buy. In study after study, when people are asked what form of advertising they trust most, the answer is always a recommendation from friends or family.

If referrals are so important, why do so many sales professionals fail to work on this important resource?

*The Sale is the Thing*

Salespeople know that their whole existence is dependent on making the sale. All of their time, energy and resources go into figuring out how to complete more sales and drive up their sales totals. Once they have gotten to the finish line and recorded that hard-won contract, many salespeople try to hit the road as quickly as possible so that the client doesn't have a chance to change their mind, snatching defeat from the jaws of victory. And, unfortunately, too many sales managers are only concerned with their sales totals, so there isn't any value placed on other parts of the sales cycle.

But referrals should be the valuable last step in any good sales process. Generating referrals can supercharge your sales department because if a client has a relationship with one of your current customers and that customer speaks highly of you, most of your sales job is done. Even if the prospect doesn't have a relationship with the person giving the referral, the fact that one of your current customers thinks highly enough of you to recommend your services is a great testament that no amount of advertising can duplicate.

## *Timing is Everything*

When should you ask for referrals? As we said earlier, when you receive a compliment from a customer is a great time to ask for a favor and that favor could be a referral. A thank you can come at several points in a customer relationship. Maybe the customer has had an interaction with your service people that they were really happy with, or they just thanked you for stopping by to chat. Buying lunch for the client's office is always appreciated, and will almost always get a 'thank you.'

At every point that your company receives a compliment or 'thank you' from the customer, make sure you follow up as soon as possible. Express your appreciation for the nice words, and ask if they would give you a recommendation. That referral can be in the form of an email that they sign, or if they're busy, jot down something based on what they said when they thanked you and offer to send it to them for approval.

Other great times to ask for referrals include when you are contacting other leads when you are at a networking or industry event or you just closed a deal with a new client. New clients are always upbeat about your business right after they sign the contract; after all, they thought enough of you to spend money with your company!

Take a look at all of your customer points of contact. Are there areas where you could also be asking for a referral? A quick note on your business cards, letterhead, and email signature is an easy way to let people know that you are always looking for help in finding great customers like them. Adding a line like "Know anyone who might benefit from my services? Reply to this email with contact info, and I'll let them know you helped them out!" is a simple way to build referral generation into all of your contact points.

If a customer doesn't have a specific referral they can give you, ask for a testimonial instead. Ask them for some feedback on what they liked about working with your company. If they give you something that you believe would help with your other customers, ask them for permission to share it with other clients. Even if this isn't a direct referral, it's still an authentic opinion that other customers will appreciate and respect.

And when you're looking for referrals, don't forget other employees at the client's company and your own company. Those other friends you've made in the customer's office work with people and have their own personal networks as well. Let them know when you see them that you would appreciate any referrals they could send your way.

### *Creating an Easy Referral System*

Building a system to create referrals is a great investment. Once you have a system that works, it will pretty much run itself. Best of all, your referral system doesn't need to be complicated. Here are the key steps in creating a referral system that will work for you:

- **Make sure you have something to refer to.** If most of your customers are unhappy, you need to work on that first. When you can easily pick up the phone and find a happy customer, you are ready to generate more referrals. Every business has a customer who didn't get what they wanted or ended things on a sour note. It happens. Just make sure that you are doing everything you can to make most of them happy.

- **Come up with a referral incentive.** Research has shown when you offer an incentive for people to give you a referral, referrals go up. Rocket science, right? Back in the day, we used to call these "spiffs." Get me a solid referral, and I'll reward you. Often, these were internal programs for employees, but you can easily offer your clients a reward, too. It doesn't have to cost a lot. Studies have shown that non-cash incentives work better than cash rewards. Remember those other businesses you were recommending in exchange for product or benefits to pass out to clients? These work for referral rewards, too. Event tickets, merchandise from partners, even a free service from your company can all work as a reward.

- **Make it easy.** The easiest way to make sure your referral program works is to make it easy for everyone involved. The simplest answer is usually the best. Print special business cards that your people can pass out with a unique tracking number. Have a simple form on a web page that can be referred to through emails and social media. Print brochures to explain the program and allow people to use it pass on to referral candidates. Once a referral code comes in, give a reward to both the new customer and the person who gave the referral. This way, you can ensure that the program will continue to generate referrals with little intervention from you. All you need to do is make sure that new customers and employees learn about the program, and the rest should take care of itself!

# Chapter 7:
## Your Sales Script Framework

**Key Points Worksheet**

The first step in developing your sales scripts is to take a moment to identify the distinct points in your specific sales funnel. There are various steps along the way and milestones that are reached at each step, either triggering the next step in the process or disqualifying that prospect from moving further. So, to get started building your scripts, ask yourself these questions:

1. What are the key points in your sales path? If these differ by product segment or customer type, write a list of key points in the process for the entire distinct sales path you have.

2. For each of the key points in all the individual paths, list the milestones that signify that the prospect has satisfied that step in the path and is ready for the next step in the process.

3. For each of the key points, also list a milestone for each that tells you that this customer isn't moving farther in the process at this point.

4. Finally, for each milestone that you listed, describe what should happen with the prospect once that milestone is reached. Do this for all of the milestones, both positive and negative.

These questions will provide you with a pathway for each of your sales channels. If you are comfortable with charting or mindmap software, consider putting these answers in a graphic that will help you visualize how the customer will move through the process.

**Breaking down the Process**

Now that you have the basic skeleton of your sales process, you can start building a strategy for each section of each of your paths. To accomplish this step in the script writing, think about the type of person you are trying to sell to in each of your distinct sales channels and how the ideal pathway would look for that sale.

To start to fill out your sales scripts for your pathway, follow these steps:

1. **Identify your target.** For each sales path, who is the ideal customer that you are looking to talk to? If the path could apply to more than one type of customer, either split that path into separate pathways for each type of buyer or consider building an "average" customer persona that incorporates most of the commonality between the different customers that could fit in one path.

2. **Name your unique value proposition (UVP) for each customer pathway.** This will be the

central theme of each script path, giving you a way to focus your scripts. While you will talk about all of your product value points in your sales process, all of the points should come back to reinforce your UVP for this type of customer.

3. **List some common problems your customers will be trying to solve.** Put together some pain points that your ideal customer is probably facing that made them call you for the solution. For each of these problems, make a brief statement of how your product solves that problem. List these problems from easy to serious. These problems should inform your scripts on how you will attempt to surface these problems so that you can sell to them. These problems might be part of your qualifying questions if they are crucial to making a customer viable.

4. **List your qualifying questions for each milestone.** Your milestones should each be triggered by increasingly specific qualifying questions. Getting the appropriate answers to these questions should move the client to the next stage in the sales cycle, so think about what you would ask a client in an interview to see if they are a fit for your product. You will want to then arrange your questions in a list, starting with the most generic questions first, then moving through to the questions that require the hardest answers. Many of your customers will be hesitant to answer some questions until they know more about you, your company and your product. Arrange your questions to take advantage of the growing familiarity with your

customer as you move through the cycle toward the sale.

5. **Word each of your milestones as a question that you can get an affirmative answer for from your prospect.** As we talked about throughout this book, building a series of "yes" answers during your sales process builds Consistency for the crucial "yes" when it comes time to close the sale.

**Writing Your Scripts**

Now that you've answered the key points of your sales paths for each type of customer or product line that you're responsible for, you have a framework to construct your selling script.

You might see a lot of gimmicky ideas when it comes to sales scripts. Many resources will give you "magic words" that get you by the gatekeepers and voice mail dungeons every time. Sliding in front of your decision maker is just a matter of giving them the right words at the right time. But if you've been selling for any length of time, you realize it doesn't quite work like that.

A good sales script is a good resource to keep you on track during the sales process, but the exact wording isn't important. Talking to a customer should sound like a natural conversation because it is. If you're going to effectively use the sales persuasion principles and techniques we've talked about in this book effectively, you will need to be listening to what your customer is telling you. If you aren't getting the answers you need, then you'll need to adjust your interview to get that information. A good sales conversation is reactive, and that is very difficult to script word-for-word.

Instead of looking at a sales script as an actual script for a play, think of it more as a road map to get you where you need to go. A map has lots of routes you can take to get to the same place. Some are very quick and easy, like a superhighway, and others are slower, winding roads with lots of stops and starts along the way. Most trips in sales will use a combination of those roads to get you to your final destination of the sale. You need to have a map ready to realize when you've gotten off track, or you're going the wrong way completely.

Depending on what you're selling, your map might cover a lot of ground, or it may just be a couple of blocks from beginning to end. Selling service subscriptions over the phone is a much different trip than selling a complex insurance strategy to a large corporate client, but they all share many of the same points in common when it comes to touching all the bases on the way to a sale.

**The Sales Funnel**

Using the information that you put together in the last section, you're going to build each of your sales funnels along the following lines. Let's start by taking a look at each main point.

*The Introduction*

This is the initial stage of the sales process, and you are simply trying to get someone interested in your product at this point. If you're lucky, you're working from a list of leads where people have already expressed an interest in your product. In this world of instant access communication through the Internet, this is thankfully getting more common.

While it used to be more difficult to get someone to take the time to make a phone call or send in a form requesting more information, a quick click on a mobile device is all that is needed to generate a lead today. The downside of this ease of connection is that most people don't put a lot of weight or thought behind that click, or they may have given you information so that they could get access to a free resource you tempted them with. So even if the lead approached your company first, don't necessarily assume that they are excited about what you're selling. Either way, you'll need to get their attention.

Your introduction should consist of the following main points, expressed as quickly and efficiently as possible:

1. Introduce yourself and your company.

2. The problem you have a solution for.

3. The qualifying question to move this prospect to the next level.

4. If you get the right answer, tell them what type of meeting you need to tell them more about your solution.

This introduction is your hook to get to the next stage, so you need to use the best stuff you've got here to create interest enough to get to the next meeting or the next stage in the process. Since this is the opening of every interaction, you can get a script that is fairly word-for-word here to get the ball rolling.

To use a sports metaphor, football coaches often use a system of starting every game with a set list of 10 plays on offense to set the stage for what they want to do the rest of the game. After that, all bets are off. Think of the introduction as your first plays to set the stage for the rest of the game.

Since this is the first contact, you will need to grab the prospect's attention. So, everything you say should be geared to how it benefits *the customer*. They aren't interested in you; they are interested in what you can do for *them*. So when you introduce yourself and the company, let them know what you are capable of doing for them. Go to your list of pain points, grab the biggest one, and tell them how you can solve that problem for them. If you have a lead form that gives you their problem of interest, use that one instead. Then tell them briefly what little you need from them to get working on that problem for them.

This first step is crucial in getting the ball rolling, and you need to make the path to this first "yes" as easy as possible. In most cases, your first agreement with the customer may be that they agree to answer a question or two while you have their attention or have them on the phone. Whatever you do, make the first step as simple as possible. By the end of this first contact, you should ideally get to set an appointment for a more in-depth meeting to get you solidly in the door to gather the real information you need.

No matter how you make your first contact, this is the one part of your sales script that you can more or less script word-for-word. Write it out and practice your opening so that you can deliver it naturally and flawlessly under pressure because this is your best hook to keep a prospect on the phone or in front of you at the door.

### *The Interview*

The interview is the next stage in the process and will give you everything you need to put together a killer presentation for the sale. For in-depth information on tips and techniques to use at this stage, see "Getting in the Door" earlier in this book.

This section is fairly straightforward in scripting, but will sometimes go in new and interesting directions once you get to the meeting. To keep that meeting on track, it's important to have a list of key questions that you want to cover. Though you won't spend a lot of time looking at these questions during the interview, you will want to glance at them from time to time during the meeting to make sure that you get all of the answers you need.

To put this part of the script together, go back to the previous worksheet section and find the qualifying question or questions that will give you the answers you need to move the client into the next level to give them a presentation to sell. You may find out during the deeper interview that the customer doesn't have the problem they told you about at first, or they don't have a problem you can solve at all. Based on your key questions, you'll need to decide whether you can create a solution that they will buy, or if they need to be gently sent in a different direction to wait until they are ready for you later. Or maybe they need someone else entirely. Your interview should be geared to find as much information as you can, but make sure that you cover the main qualifying questions in the process, so you know if they trigger the next milestone in the process.

Again, it's important to understand that you are still not selling your solution. You are gaining the information you need for your presentation so that you can design the right sell for this customer. Your goals for this part of the script are to qualify the customer for the presentation, get the information you need for an effective presentation, and get agreement for the next meeting.

### *The Sales Presentation and Close*

This is where you will once again have a script going in where you will be able to start more or less in a direction that you have pre-written and practiced. You need to control this meeting from start to finish as much as possible because both you and the client realize that this meeting is about you and your solution. The prospect is waiting to see what you can do for them, and you need to deliver on the promise you made to them way back in the first contact in the most powerful and efficient way possible. Depending on what you're selling, this could be a simple presentation of the offer, or it could be a well thought out plan covering many different components that your company offers to solve the customer's needs.

While you won't be able to write your presentation now, you will be able to start collecting components of presentations that you can reuse to assemble each one, based on what you learn from the sales interview. Never throw out a presentation! Everyone can be a learning experience, even if it is only a lesson on what *not* to do. Save the parts that work the best and reuse them for similar situations in the future.

Also, make yourself a note at each point in your presentation to ask for the sale. You may have the greatest presentation of all time planned, but if the customer is ready to sign after your first couple of points, then sign! You can get the rest of the necessary information to him after you have the check. When you are into the final path toward the sale, you should always be looking for the right time to close the sale. You don't need to wait to the end.

### *Handling Objections and Close Again*

If you don't make the sale happen immediately, it will be because you've run into an objection or two. Using the sections of this book on "Killing the Presentation" and "Negotiating the Deal," make some bullet points in this part of your script on how to handle some of the most common objections using the LAER model — Listen, Acknowledge, Explore and Respond.

This is another section where you will have little control over the exact way in which this stage goes, but you will always be looking to bring the conversation back around to closing the sale.

## *After the Sale*

Don't forget this part of your script. You need to make sure that you attend to the client after the sale to make sure they're happy, to build your relationship going forward so that you may be able to sell them again in the future and mine them for additional business referrals to keep your sales funnel full of new prospects.

As you begin customizing this step for yourself, you'll want to script out your steps to make sure you have this customer set up so that you will always be in contact.

## Example Script

Here is an example script workup for a sales path to selling replacement windows to homeowners who have requested more information. Combining the Key Points Worksheet and a Script Framework, you can see how you can assemble a process for any product you may be selling.

### 1. Identify the Target

Customer looking to replace three or more windows in their home. Customer must own their home and have a budget of $750 or more, depending on the size of the project.

### 2. Unique Value Proposition (UVP)

XYZ Window and Door has a quick process that can have most windows installed in a day or less, regardless of the number. This keeps the disruption to your home at an absolute minimum.

### 3. Typical Problems for this Customer

- Wants an affordable price.

- Wants windows to add value to the home.

- Wants energy and noise reductions with new windows.

- Wants the process to be easy.

### 4. Qualifying Questions

- How many windows do you need to replace?

- Are you getting the home ready for sale, or are you planning on keeping it for several years?

- How soon do you need replacements?

- What is your budget?

### 5. Milestone questions

- Would you like to me to come and do a free analysis of your window needs?

- Can I come back tomorrow afternoon with some options that will take care of your needs, or would tomorrow evening be better?

- With those suggestions, would like to go with our [top level windows at just above budget], or our [next step down product within budget]?

# The Script

## *Milestone 1: First Contact*

Hi! This is Ryan Smith with XYZ Window and Door. Is this _____?

You had contacted us about helping you get rid of the old, drafty windows in your home. Tell me a little about what windows need to be replaced.

[This turns the conversation to be about them as quickly as possible. For our first milestone, we're looking for 3 or more windows to replace. Less than that, and we refer to a handyman who buys windows from us to do small jobs.]

That sounds perfect. We have an exclusive replacement system that will have all of those windows replaced and weather-tight in a day or less. We'll remove and dispose of all of the old windows for no additional charge, and leave your home as clean as we found it. Does that sound good?

[Start getting agreement]

I need about an hour of your time to measure all of the windows you need to be replaced and to gather a little information so I can put together a quote for you. Are you available [first available time], or would [second available time] work out better for me to stop by?

[work out the appointment]

Excellent. As I said, my name is Ryan, and my company, XYZ Window and Door, has been doing business in your neighborhood for over ten years. I'll be by at [appointment time]. Are there any other questions you have right now?

[briefly answer questions, promise more information when visiting]

Okay. I won't keep you any longer! See you [appointment time].

## *Milestone 2: Measurement Meeting*

Key question list:

Does customer own their home?

Who else needs to make the decision?

Are you getting the home ready to sell, or are you planning to live here for a while?

Do we sell windows that will fit this project?

Do we have installation available in the required time frame?

What is the approximate budget for the project, and is it realistic?

What are the most important factors for your new windows?

[Affirmative answers to these questions move to the next milestone. Make sure we have answers to all before setting a time for the sales presentation]

I've got everything I need right now, [First name]. I would like to do a little research to make sure I've got the best options for your windows, and come back to go over the pricing with [all people who need to sign off on the decision] and see if we can get you started soon. Would tomorrow evening work well, or is there a better time?

## *Milestone 3: The Presentation*

Put together presentations on two price levels of windows for the project. First one presented should be at a price level just above the customer's stated budget. Sell features that pertain to the key factors the customer gave you during the measurement meeting.

Prepare second price level option to present if the first option is not going to work for the customer. Use this level to overcome price objection, and give the smaller asking price a better chance after the turn down on the higher ask.

- Close the sale.

- Sign contracts.

- Set starting appointment.

- Collect deposit.

## *Milestone 4: After the sale*

Schedule time to visit home when the installation crew arrives. Introduce crew to the homeowner and answer any questions that may have come up before beginning the project. Turn the project over to the installation crew and leave your contact information for the homeowner to call if any questions arise during the installation.

After installation complete, come back to the home and inspect work, assure satisfaction with work and collect the remainder of the payment.

Thank the customer, and if the customer is happy with work, tell them about our referral program.

Schedule follow-ups to touch base in 3 months to make sure the customer is happy and ask again for referrals and testimonial letters. Offer information on our other home improvement services. Ask if the customer would like our free monthly email newsletter.

Schedule semi-annual notes to thank them for their purchase and remind them about the referral program.

**Wrapping Up**

That's the process, all scripted and easy to follow so you don't miss a beat. Use this script as a template for your own sales scripting. You may have more or fewer milestones, depending on what you're selling and the complexity of the final offer, but this is a good model to start with for most any industry.

Use the information in the appropriate sections of this book to refine and build your scripts over time so you turn them into selling machines that you can replicate over and over again to implement all the tools of the psychology of selling and persuasion that we have outlined here.

I wish you profitable selling!

# Conclusion

We have attempted to cover the best and most important research and practices associated with the modern profession of sales, but there is more research on the subject being done every day.

In addition to the studies being done to understand human behavior, there are new media to study. Social media, email, video messaging, online shopping and more have been around for a relatively short period of time, yet these technologies have rocked the world of marketing, advertising and sales like nothing else since the advent of printing presses and later, the broadcast mediums of radio and television.

How will these new mediums work together to create the new sales systems of tomorrow is anyone's guess. But one thing won't change. People are still people, and they make the ultimate decisions on purchasing. The foundational research on the psychology of selling and persuasion that we have outlined here has been true since trading was born, and it will stay at the base of buying behavior no matter what comes tomorrow.

We hope you will continue to find this information useful, no matter what the future brings to the future of sales. If you enjoyed this book, please give us a rating and review on Amazon to help others find *The Psychology of Selling and Persuasion*.

**Other Books by Leonard Moore**

Do you want to learn how to read, analyze and influence other people? The truth is… our bodies say many things about us, before we even speak a word. By looking at somebody's facial expressions, hand gestures and body language you can understand his feelings, the motives behind his actions, and sometimes even his thoughts. Just think about all the ways you could use this knowledge in your advantage. And the best part is, reading people isn't some kind of vague nonsense, it's a practice that's actually based on science and psychology.

If you want to learn how to read people, understand their behavior and influence them, this is the book for you. In this book, you'll learn how to analyze people on the spot using science-based techniques. You'll learn the meanings of expressions and microexpressions, hand movements, verbal and non-verbal clues, leg movements, personality types and human behavior in general. The problem with books on this subject is that reading them feels like reading bad textbooks. They will only talk about the theory, but will never show you how to actually apply what you're learning. This book is different. After learning all the techniques and secrets to read people like a pro, you'll find a collection of examples that will show you how to analyze people in real life scenarios. You'll also learn 12 "FBI Style" strategies for reading people instantly.

Inside How to Analyze People, discover:
- Science based techniques to analyze people and understand their motives, thoughts and emotions.
- Seemingly innocuous questions you can ask to understand somebody's personality and feelings.
- 12 FBI Style strategies for instantly reading people without them knowing what you're doing.
- The 13 most common hand movements you can study to understand thoughts, feelings, and emotions.
- Why and how you should be reading verbal clues to understand motives, behavior and personality.
- 27 psychology based tips to spot a liar (that actually work).
- A step-by-step process to determine a person's personality type by asking yourself a set of questions.

- Practical examples of how to read people in real life scenarios.
- Why you shouldn't look at standalone signs if you want to analyze body language (and what you should be doing instead).
- The #1 indicator you should analyze to read and understand emotions without letting anybody know that you're doing it.

Even if you have no clue about psychology and human behavior, this book will give you all the tools you need to read people and better understand their motives, thoughts and emotions.

**"How to Analyze People" by Leonard Moore is available on Amazon.**

# HYPNOSIS

Learn the Secret Techniques and the Exact Hypnotic Scripts to Persuade and Control Anyone using Hypnosis

## LEONARD MOORE

Do you want to learn how to actually hypnotize people? Hypnosis isn't what most people think… Yes, hypnosis is real, but it isn't a magical way to make people do what you want. Neither it is a stage show, as some may make it out to be. This practice has been surrounded by mystery and false ideas for centuries, but the truth is that hypnosis is actually a very scientific process you can follow.

You see… hypnosis, the real hypnosis, is a natural phenomenon that can be harnessed to talk to somebody's subconscious mind and guide his decisions and actions, but most importantly it's also a skill that can be developed.

If you want to learn the real techniques to hypnotize other people, then this book is for you. In this book you'll learn how to hypnotize a person following a science based process that actually works. You'll learn everything about wording, hypnotic voice, scripts, body language, hypnotic induction and more.

You'll also discover the history of hypnosis, what's true, what's false and the different methods and procedures. This guide includes detailed instructions to help you build your own effective scripts to hypnotize other people, even if you've never done it before..

Inside Hypnosis you'll discover:
- An effective process you can follow to hypnotize a subject, keep him/her into trance and speak to his/her subconscious mind
- Common myths demystified (including "only people with low intelligence can be hypnotized" and "you can be hypnotized anytime/anywhere")
- Why we're all in trance very often without even noticing it and how you can take advantage of this to hypnotize others
- This small change in your voice can make a big difference the next time you hypnotize someone
- What are all the stages of an effective hypnosis session
- 5 things that can make a person more likely to fall in a hypnotic trance
- How to take advantage of a common natural phenomenon to successfully hypnotize people
- The #1 rule to follow when constructing an effective script to hypnotize people
- The history of hypnosis, from mysterious practice to stage show to scientific process

- Practical examples of what to say to induce hypnotic trance in your subject

And much, much more...

Even if you're starting from scratch, you'll learn how to perform an effective hypnosis session, including how to induce trance, how to talk to the subconscious mind and how to wake up your subjects.

**"Hypnosis" by Leonard Moore is available on Amazon.**

Printed in Great Britain
by Amazon